Table Of Contents

All The Answers
Sex, Love, Relations

Introduction: @trapsamceph

Before we go any further I would like to introduce myself to those of you that don't know. My name is Sam Cephas hailing from Brooklyn, New York and I done seen it all. The money the power the streets and the luxuries of life but most importantly I've cheated death with the grace of God. From being shot, to a near fatal car accident only to recover and almost lose my life again.

After 60 months in Federal custody for pleading guilty as a co-conspirator to a $1.5 million jewelry store heist. I promised myself and family to stop living life on the edge. Throughout those 60 months incarcerated I've maintained relationships with several women including my ex-wife while taking therapeutic online relationship courses and over the course of time I've gotten them all to do just exactly what I wanted them to do for me.

During my incarceration I began studying people. From the men I lived amongst to the female officers and women on the outside I used for companionship. As I progressed many felons whom I known from the streets would come to me for advice about their relationships with their wives, girlfriends and fiancés. Often after utilizing my advice, they would all return to me with good news. It became overwhelming, prisoners would approach me with all different types of questions, usually "asking for a friend." I then began increasing the prices for my services.

With consistently having a cell full of cosmetics, and commissary that molded I started to give it to the less fortunate. I then formulated my second business, I began asking for wire transfers for a several hundred dollars. In return I would type poems, give relationship advice, and for $1000 I would have flowers mailed out to their companions residents. 16 months in many of my contacts on the inside and outside would refer to me as Dr. Love or the relationship expert. I then felt the need to live up to these expectations, not only does my present and many previous relationships qualifies for these titles, but I also have the credentials to prove it. So now that you know a little bit about me, I want you all to get to know your companions a lot better and in the process you'll see if they know you as good as you think you do.

Have you ever participated in a survey? Well you're not the only one, but have you ever conducted a survey? If not then here's your chance, don't worry this will be interesting as well as easy. I challenge you all to write down 10-25 questions about yourself that you think your spouse should know about you. These questions can be sexual, mental, or physical just don't be surprised at the answers you receive, and try not to react irrational.

If you are single, you can still participate but you might want to save these questions for your new relationship. Here's a few questions to get you started.

"What's the one thing I like most about being in a relationship with you?"

"If we only had time for a quickie before work, what position would we be in?"

"How many times a day would I like to have sex if our schedules allowed us to?"

"How many children do I want?" "What's my favorite ice cream?" "What do I prefer to watch, horror, crime/mystery, or comedy?"

Questions like these would allow you to understand how well your mate knows you and the things you may need your mate to know, as well as work improve in.

Before we continue I would like to share a couple must do's for you to try to abide by even though we all know that "rules are made to be broken"

Must Do #1: Get your life in order before you order someone new into your life!

It's difficult to establish a good bond with someone else if your life is in chaos. If your life is out of order then your knew relationships will be just as chaotic, unless you meet someone who's willing to assist you with your chaos. Are you willing to except a new person in your life that comes with already made baggage, mayhem, or turmoil? You aren't the only one, most wouldn't!

Don't Do #2: Never settle for less than your expectations!

If you meet someone then find out that are unqualified for what you expect or want in a companion then walk away. Don't settle because the sex is good, or because you can use them as a financial crutch. Instant gratification often leads to a lifetime of misery.

Must Do #3: Speak your mind at all times!

When you disagree or dislike something about a situation, state how you feel at that time. Don't bottle things up, the more you harbor your thoughts and feelings the more likely you are to overreact at a later time. Holding in your thoughts and opinions about negative encounters are like volcanos waiting to erupt.

Chapter 1:
Simplify Communication

A common belief is that communication is the key to a happy and healthy relationship. When I speak of communication I don't just mean calling your mate on their cell phone and asking them, "How's your day going?" Though the simplicity of those kind of casual phone calls can assist with building long-lasting relationships. When sincere, these forms of communication can lead to organic climaxes. A relationship can become tumultuous if calls are being made with motives that question your companion whereabouts! Communicating about your expectations should come naturally. If you expect monogamy you should communicate that by your actions but be sure that the desire is reciprocated. Instead of calling and interrogating be straight forward and tell them what you want and need, but only after showing your position first.

Even if your mate do decide that they would like to be in an exclusive relationship, please try not to become overprotective and possessive. Don't question their every action just to assure yourself that they are being monogamous, because insecurity looks ugly on everyone no matter how beautiful you are. No one wants to be interrogated, belittled, and accused of wrong, especially when they have been faithful all along.

As time progress being possessive may lead to combative arguments, resulting in abusive relationship. Some people do like the idea that their mate cares or love them enough to want to keep tabs on them, but not to the point of a nuisance. If your mate at some point becomes this annoying partner, please do address your issues. Find a polite way to communicate your thoughts and feelings about things that you are not pleased with. Sooner or later, the small issues become big issues which is always problematic.

Have you ever had a co-worker, neighbor, client, or associate that complained about car trouble but continued to delay the trip to the auto mechanic? Then that one day their vehicle breaks down while in traffic on the highway, killing themselves and several others, during the two dozen car pileup which stalls rush hour traffic for five hours. Well, if you haven't encountered someone that this has happened to, then consider yourself fortunate. This collision is equivalent to what can happen in relationships where companions keep issues that they have with their mate all bottled up without addressing the situation. As time progress, these issues will spiral out of control, taking a toll on both parties. Releasing intense frustration often result in a physical altercation where feelings and anatomies are hurt, injured or worst.

Communication is always work in progress, companions should never stop communicating. Communicating is key as long as you're willing to make the relationship work. Communication is involved with just about all aspects in a relationship even during sex, but it doesn't have to always be said in words. Ones feelings and thoughts can be corresponded through action, facial expressions, body language, or other specific signs without verbal acknowledgement. Sex is where some women go wrong with corresponding. Faking orgasms, pretending to be pleased, when you're not or acting as if he or she is doing something right when in reality, it's all wrong. What is pleasing to one, may be displeasing to another!

Honesty may not always be the best policy, except when it comes to sex. What do you prefer? To be pleased? Or to have your mate thinking he/she is doing the right thing but knowing they're not? By relaying a message through body language that you're not pleased, can happen in many ways. For instance, signs can be shown by a blank stare, a sigh, a roll of the eyes, clenching your legs closed, lack of participation, laying there staring at the ceiling or simply stopping your mate in progress. All these scenarios would trigger the inquiry of "what's wrong?" Which would lead to your honesty!

Start by telling your companion that you're not intending to be mean, hurtful or rude but you're just not being pleased the way you deserve to be. Next, you should look them in their eyes, if you're not doing so already, followed by a passionate hug and kiss. Then tell them what you want and guide them to performing all the right moves you like, in order to be properly pleased. Remember, the longer you prolong telling the truth, the deeper you fall into living a lie.

Great correspondence is not only beneficial when it comes to sex, it is in fact needed to live a stress free, drama reduced life. If your companion agrees to pay the electric bill and car note every month, but you read mail that states otherwise, don't wait until the lights get turned off and the vehicle is repossessed in order for you to confront your mate with neglecting their responsibilities. You should start leaving friendly reminders of the notices from bills on the refrigerator door and wait for the response. If the issue continues to be avoided, then politely mention it over dinner. If the excuse is fair, think of a legitimate alternative to making sure all bills are paid before things escalate and an argument ensues. Keep in mind, it's not what you say but how you say it.

You attract more flies with honey than vinegar so for those men and women out there that would like a threesome, don't flat out ask for one in a manner so enthused that it seems that you prefer a threesome at all cost, even at the expense of your relationship. Don't allow your fantasies to cost you your relationship, if it's not asked the right way then you'll never get your threesome. Instead, don't be overzealous but be patient about it. Slowly inquire about your companion's fantasies, maybe you'l find out that they've been fantasizing about the same thing all along.

If their fantasy is not the same, let them in on your fantasy of a threesome. Try after a racy sexual encounter where both adrenalines are pumping. Say something like, "Wow that was amazing, you feel so good and you look so sexy when we're making love, we should have someone film us?" If they agree then you add your preference casually like, "Preferably a woman can film us and after maybe she could join in?" This statement would open up a broad topic of discussion, allowing you both to express your views about being filmed and most importantly, your threesome. If the conversation goes left, you can always blame it on the "alcohol" or the adrenaline rush then regroup for a new strategy, though my belief is if you were pleasing your mate the right way, they'll agree to whatever you like after having a thrilling orgasm.

When one is in a state of sexual excitement, the mind and body is overwhelmed with bliss, often causing your mate to agree with you without giving second thought to the question or statement made. Persuading someone to a future commitment to fulfill your every fantasy may feel a bit manipulative, but what's really fare when it comes to pleasure? Technically it's not total manipulation, I would define it as strategic. Asking the right question, or making the right statement, at the right time, for the right response. Sort of like asking someone for something, when you know they're inebriated and in a good mood. As stated earlier, there's many ways to communicate, you just have to learn the right technique for the right person. If being under the influence of an orgasm or alcohol does not work, then get more creative.

Speaking to someone and using body language are not the only forms in which we communicate. My belief is that another effective way of communication goes without saying. Our actions literally speak louder than our words and it's the little words that mean a whole lot. Most women I encountered loved when I left them messages like, "I love you" "thinking of you" "I'm in love with the love of my life" or similar messages left on their bedroom or bathroom mirror. In return, they would send me a sexy picture with a sexy text message attached. I enjoy being fed while they sit in lingerie during a candle lit dinner. Three day getaway's with surprised threesomes would always be my favorite. In return, I'll take them to their favorite place to relax, usually "Spa Castle" where we do nothing but relax, think of peace and prosperity while enjoying one another's company. Quite often in order to get people to treat you how you want to be treated you have to teach them.

Though leaving my ex-wife messages by any means, expressing my thoughts of her, or sending roses to her job was not much. Those little things prompted thoughts that may have been unfulfilled had I not taken the steps to receive such responses. Our actions display indications of our thoughts. Being that our actions also express our emotions, those of you that "wear your hearts on your sleeve" are seen through your emotions. Whether it's considered good or bad, it depends on you and your mate. A lot of times you're often criticized by showing your emotions when hit with phrases such as, "You're so emotional!" "Your always in your feelings" Besides the things you say, emotions are shown by the way you treat people after corresponding. Just because you and your companion had a small disagreement, doesn't mean you have to sneak and take the keys to the vehicle you bought them. Your actions can show that you may be immature or unforgiving. Just because someone disagrees with you, you shouldn't become angered and feel the need to be spiteful.

It's okay to agree to disagree and let things be. For every action there's a reaction but you may not be ready for the repercussions. I'm all the way anti domestic violence! For most God fearing people we know the word states we should be slow to anger, which I interpret as we should not make decisions when we're in our feelings or in an emotional state. Most bad decisions happen when we're angry, and even in that moment we know it's the wrong choice to make. Decisions made without giving much thought without sex involved usually has the opposite effect that the sexual excitement brings. It would be compatible to making a sexual decision when one is sexually frustrated.

Acting off emotions is not always bad if your actions are coming from a place of good intentions because of the love you have for your mate. When there's a small or big quarrel between you and your mate it is best to resolve it immediately if you plan on having a future together. "All couples have disagreements" no matter who you are, from Jay Z & Beyonce to Michelle and Barack Obama. Forgiving someone can be expressed many ways and this can be the best time to allow your actions to speak. How about doing something special for your mate like surprising them with a gift? Or out on a date to somewhere romantic, fun and exciting. Or maybe roundtrip, all inclusive tickets to that country you two have been fantasizing about. These choices depend on how much you forgive them, your future plans together and of course how elated and excited you want them to be. Surprising someone with something joyous when they're feeling wronged, humiliated, frustrated and sad, leads to an overwhelming feeling of bliss. Usually this results in great make up sex, replacing these sad feelings with orgasmic experiences. Due to all the emotions involved from both parties often leads to a stronger, emotional, mental, and physical connection.

After a few quarrels are forgiving with gifts, trips and great sex, one mate usually takes the lead, becoming the thinker of the relationship. As time progress, grabbing your companion in the midst of a disagreement, hugging them tightly, interrupting in mid-sentence with a passionate kiss followed by the words "I love you" often leads to premature make up sex.

Overtime, these same actions that ends with blissful results, comes organically and the makeup sex starts before an argument even ensues. Not to say that great sex is the answer to all of our relationship issues but knowing your mate, having great chemistry and being able to agree to disagree, allows us to express our emotions more freely, reacting with emotions that come from a good place where love resides and not a place of malice.

Getting to know your mate is only half of the battle, knowing how to deal with them is the other. Knowing your mate is another key component to a happy long-term relationship, full of excitement, lots of fun, romance and great sex. For instance, if your mate happens to be a nurse who works 8-12 hour shifts, constantly walking up and down the hospital corridors, then coming home early, cooking her dinner and making her a warm bubble bath followed by a foot massage or full body massage, would relieve all her stress, plus show how much you care. The feeling of being pampered after a long day at work is priceless.

Ladies, please be assured that if your mate works hard or even if he makes easy money but provides for you and is trying his best to please you, then you should reciprocate that love. If your relationship isn't going according to plan then now is the best time to correct any issues and get it all in proper perspective. Yes, the truth sometimes hurt and it can also set you free. Free from the burden of thinking things will change in your relationship, when they usually don't, unless you address the issues. I suggest you start by expressing to your mate your dislikes along with ways to improve your companionship. Secretly set a date in your mind, giving your mate enough time to change their ways and if they don't comply then you know it may be time to plan your exit. Or be prepared to remain in an unhappy relationship, where things will most likely get worst before they get better.

Getting to know your mate is a part of progressing. Understanding your mate facial expressions, and body language is a bonus. Those small expressions is the most common way people communicate without actually saying how they feel or what's on their mind. Figuring out your companion body language and facial expressions is another class all by itself because first you would have to understand your companion mind. No, I don't mean literally reading their mind. I'm referring to understanding their mindset, their way of thinking, their ideologies on different aspects of life. If you don't know already, I suggest you find out soon. In this case, it doesn't hurt to ask. Asking is one of the ways that you're going to find out how they view things which plays a major role in their actions and reactions throughout your relationship.

For instance, how does your mate view his mother? Categorizing her as "old school or old fashion" prior to you meeting her? If so then on the day you're going to meet her, you may want to wear something less revealing than that tight short dress to show off your nice figure that you've been working on at the gym. If you would've put on that sexy dress then most likely he would have suggested for you to take it off and change, which would have led to a disagreement. Which probably would have resulted in great make up sex! When you know your mate, you start to make decisions that you both would be happy with to avoid as many disagreements as possible. The fact that no one is perfect is the reason why there will be spats and quarrels, it's just in the human nature of building a relationship. One of the main keys to a blissful relationship is limiting the disagreements to the least possible.

No one wants to walk on eggshells just to appease their mate, but less arguing leaves more time for romance, sex, fun and excitement. In all dynamics of companionships, it is great to know your mate and anything you don't know, it is best not to avoid discussing. Cut to the chase and ask. You want to make sure that you're on the same page. For example, when out dining, one should know the little things like what foods your partner are allergic to. Or does this establishment only accept debit cards or cash, such things may seem so minuscule but after a few alcoholic beverages, these small things can lead to a big argument. Believe me, I know! I've encountered these types of situations and worst. Unfortunately I learned the embarrassing way like surprising an ex-girlfriend with a birthday party at a restaurant where I fed her butter pecan ice cream, with her pecan pie, only to find out that she was allergic to pecans which ruined the entire surprise party and the whole night for that matter. In fact, now that I think about it, that one incident caused us to part our separate ways.

What you don't know about your companion can ultimately dismantle the relationship you already built. What you've just grown to like becomes a distant memory. Yes, even the good things about that person which brought out your inner feelings. Getting to know your mate is similar to preparing for a test. Think of the test as the major disagreements you may encounter to avoid these small disputes. Limit them as early as possible or risk the struggle of keeping them from spiraling out of control. In order to do so, you have to study your companion. Similar to studying the subject matter, prior to taking the exam. You have to learn your mate's likes, dislikes, wants, needs and how to treat your' mate, especially in public. Learning your companion facial expressions, and actions under pressure would make every experience pleasurable. Stress relievers, daily routines, behaviors and mood swings is essential, but remembering the right things, at the right time will always keep you a step ahead of what's to come.

Abnormal patterns in daily schedules and behaviors are huge signs that there is something wrong, not necessarily in the relationship itself, maybe just in the individual. Whether its stemming from the stress at work, receiving low pay for laborious hours or an illness in her family, her mother may have been diagnosed with breast cancer or her father may have been diagnosed with a chronic disease and is predicted to have a limited time left here on earth. I know what you're possibly thinking, "Why should I have to figure out what's wrong with her/him why can't they just tell me?" Often people react in many different ways during times of sadness. They may not be in their right state of mind due to stress, some may prefer not to put their stress or burdens on their companion.

Stress can cause people to act abnormal, develop mood swings, express anger towards those closest to them with verbal abuse or simply shutting down. If these signs constantly exist with your significant other, I suggest you do a thorough investigation because in some cases, these are all indications of a cheating companion. Is your mate cheating? Here are a few signs. Secretive phone calls! You know, those phone calls he can't seem to make with you staring him in the eyes. Finding charges on his debit/credit card bill that are unaccounted for, like small bills for $300 here and there. If you don't have all the information about what was purchased then you need to find this information immediately. She could be using that $300 on hotels, while you're thinking she's at work. You maybe stuck, wondering why she claim to have used up all of her sick days and even those are unaccounted for! Most common is when you call your mate several times and she refuses to answer, then hours later she calls you back claiming she left her phone at work or a friend's house. I forgot my phone in the car, the ringer was off, or similar excuses are signs of cheating. "Should I go cheat as well?" Maybe, but we'll get into that in another chapter.

The most popular way of concealing an affair is when your mate has a secret phone that he doesn't want you to know about. Maybe that's the unknown monthly charge on his debit/credit card bill, that you've been inquiring about.

Above are all scenarios that may occur, so what's a person to do? Do you,

A. Confront your mate with the evidence to see whether they confess or not, and you leave them anyway?

B. Confront your mate and whether or not they confess you forgive, and move forward?

C. Avoid confrontation, and step it up all around the board. Meaning, you don't allow room for them to cheat. "How I'm supposed to do that?" one may ask.

It's now time to start surprising your companion, showering them with your attention, affection and love. Wait, before you dive in, be sure that your mate is really into you, the same way that you're into them! Okay, if they're not exactly into you as much as you're into them because the relationship is still fresh, or you're working out some issues. Here's how you get them fully into you.

If you're done with your schedule early on a Friday then surprise them at their work place or school. Bring them something they really like then take them to their favorite place whether it's the statute of liberty or a sex party. Then again Saturday, may just be better. Start your Saturday off early, try to spend a night together at whichever place is more convenient. If you can sneak out of bed early and make breakfast do so. Taste it first to make sure that it is up to standards, if breakfast pass the taste test then bring it to your companion on the best dishes available. Gently awaken your companion with a few soft kisses, allow them to slowly awake, don't scare them out of their sleep "we all hate that, don't we!" Once they're awake, allow them the opportunity to quickly freshen up (take care of their personal hygiene) then welcome them back to bed, allowing them to relax.

After propping up your companions upper back and head with those fluffy pillows, make sure they are comfortable. Then proceed to slowly feed them that delicious breakfast that you've just prepared. Why breakfast? Some may ask. Breakfast is the most important meal of the day because it is the first meal eaten after the longest period of time that your body goes without having food. It's also the meal that has the most effect on the body replenishing. Which assist the brain to act more effectively "Becoming more alert" Your mate now acknowledges your beauty and how you're catering and pampering them, through this most vulnerable time of day! Just another moment, you're not done just yet. Now that you have your companions mind and body working as one, it is time to take full advantage of their anatomy. Particularly their sexual organs! You have them right where you want them, well rested, partially full, alert, and hopefully undressed. Start with the neck, under to the left or right side of the chin, slowly suck and kiss that sensitive area while caressing their genitals. Please excuse me for getting a step ahead of myself. I'll give you the sexual details about how to please your mate in another chapter. For now, just make sure that you sexually stimulate your mate before continuing the day and if you don't know how! Then I suggest that you don't delay reading the remainder of this book, so you can study the sexual details.

After sexually pleasuring your mate it's time to handle your hygiene. Lather your wash rags in your best smelling soap, after running that warm bubble bath while bathing your mate, express to them your feelings. Adding just enough pressure to their neck, back and shoulders will relieve some tenseness. Even if you don't massage well this whole experience will be overwhelming, stimulating their mind and body. These types of pampering techniques forms a calm state of being, which in most cases rises the libido. Now that the libido is raised, should you take advantage of your mates sex drive, indulging in round two of sexual pleasures? Or should you simply rinse off, dry your bodies and get dressed in your best for the occasion that you have planned? Well, the answer to this question lies within, your urges, your drives, your intentions. Though you are the one doing the pleasing and appeasing, you're also the one doing the teasing because you are in total control.

Make sure you and your mate are dressed for the occasion, or you may find yourself in a compromising position. For instance, if his favorite thing to do is bowl and you want to surprise him with a bowling party, please don't wear heels and a mini skirt. Maybe a mini skirt minus the heels. We all agree that mini skirts are sexy and so are high heels but when you bend over to bowl do you want the whole party to get a peek at your goodies? Are you the no panty type? The heels of course can be switched with bowling shoes but after you've played a couple games of bowling, the last thing you want to do is put some heels back on. You're going to want to be as comfortable as possible, after lifting that weighted ball, squatting, bending over and tossing that bowling ball numerous times. Sure, this may not be the most romantic date but tonight it's all about your mate and if bowling isn't something you love to do but he/she does, then pick something you both like doing. Be sure to experience some place romantic after you're done.

You're going in with the intentions of showing that you're the one, and she needs to pay more attention to you. Take her someplace that she's never been before. How about a helicopter ride over the city at night, when the sky line is illuminated from all of the cities lights. Prior to the ride, make sure you purchase her favorite dessert along with a dozen roses. In the future when she reminisces about this night, she'll have the taste for the red velvet cake that you fed her for dessert and the urge to smell roses. You've just added a scent and a taste as she reminisce on this beautiful view.

When we make dates for our mates, it should be either some place they love going and doing or something that would leave them in awe. Having that wow moment every time they share their memorable experiences with their girlfriends is priceless. As the night comes to an end whether it ends at your place, her place or a hotel, it is wise to perform oral sex on your companion before or even after sexual intercourse preferably before. This is when you take the time out to let your mate know that it's all about them. I suggest you come across subtle, while they're in the shower or bath. You should dim the lights or turn the lights completely off. Replacing the darkness with a glow of scented candle lights, apple cinnamon is my favorite. What's yours? When your companion is done, allow them to join you in bed, start off slow with gentle touches, leading to soft kisses on the neck, licking up to their lips, transpiring your licks into a tongue kiss. As you caress their skin, continue kissing, allowing your passion for them to be felt through your affection. Turn your attention back to their soft skin, kissing, licking and sucking every inch of their body. Yes, every single inch.

Subsequent to 15 minutes of foreplay, your mate should be extremely sexually excited, as her body craves sexual satisfaction. Gently lay her on her back and spread her legs apart in order to expose her saturated vagina. Use your tongue to slowly lick her vaginal lips in a circular motion, around the entire perimeter of her vagina. Slowly glide your hands up her outer thighs across her hips until you reach her breast, which you should caress simultaneously in the same motion with your tongue. Maintain consistency with your fingers, caressing her areola's while using your tongue to circulate across her clitoris (located at the upper end of the vulva). Brace yourself, your tongue thrusting against her erectile organ will cause her body to tense up, as you stimulate her sexually.

She may react spontaneously with reflexes of a cat, clasping your body intensely, usually your head, neck or shoulders. Relax, this sort of reaction is normal, disregard her tight grip on you and concentrate on what's literally staring you in the face (her sweet smelling vagina). As you stroke your tongue against her clit repeatedly, her moans may grow louder and longer or both. This is her way of communicating to you that her body is being sexually stimulated and the sensations are increasing. Now that her body is talking to you, it is imperative that you reply without uttering a word. Suck her clitoris while rotating your tongue against it and rubbing her nipples with your finger tips. Her clasp may get tighter and her moans may get louder but don't stop, continue sucking and licking her clit, slowly increasing the pace as your own erection grows unattended. Continue to release your sexual frustration on your mate by aggressively sucking her clitoris, thrusting your tongue harder across it, at a rapid pace non stop. If done right, within minutes your mate would be proliferating orgasms consecutively, but be prepared for what's next to come.

It's been proven that performing oral sex on a woman the right way, can have her feeling in a way that she's never felt before which can have a lasting effect on her mentally and emotionally, but this may just be what you want. Rumor has it, a way to a woman's heart is through her vagina and of course through romance and shivery. Now that your task is complete, you should have your companions undivided attention. In fact, she should now be into you more than ever before and don't be surprised if at the end of the night, she utters those 3 words that some couples randomly tell each other even when they don't really mean it, "I Love You".

Love, what does it really mean? How do you know you're in it? As defined in the (Webster's New World College Dictionary, LOVE a deep and tender feeling and affection for, or devotion to a person or persons. An expression of ones love or affection. Strong usually passionate, affection of one person for another, based in part on sexual affection.)

Then again on second thought I guess if most of our young couples are using the word Love described as in the third part of this definition, then they just may very well mean it. These days most lovers seem to be on conditional terms and being faithful, loyal, monogamous and trustworthy is just about a thing of the past. During my Federal incarceration at one point my wife of seven years stated to me "you're locked up, so there's nothing you can do for me." Partially correct, I respected my wife's opinion and as my phone calls and letters sent to her gradually diminished, I came to the realization that her love for me was conditional. Our relationship was based on the condition that I provided financially, emotionally, mentally, physically while stimulating her sexually. As an imprisoned man I was unable to meet my wife's needs but spiritually and mentally, I was at a place that advanced me beyond my years. 3 years in I continued my mental, and financial support. My wife became distant and as her visits became less frequent she did just enough to remain an asset. I then decided to reach out to other Women to handle the task my wife once fulfilled.

Most people are content with the basic information they've acquired, and at times apprehensive to learn new things because learning new things is usually a challenge. Tara was different, she was excited to speak with me daily to learn new things. As I challenged Tara intellectually, she became fascinated with my logic, which resulted in her making unscheduled visits. Tara's surprised visits was short lived when she met Chelsea unexpectedly waiting to visit one December afternoon.

After having several conversations using three way calls with Tara and Chelsea I was able to guide them both with understanding that if they visit me together they would both have more time with me. Once Tara and Chelsea formed their bond and we was on one accord I was able to take my mind off of my wife which is where I found my solace. Mentally I've gained an enormous amount of knowledge, due to studying psychology immensely. I then was able to guide Tara and Chelsea mentally, physically, financially and emotionally. Which soon resulted in me directing my new acquaintances to excessive wealth. Time progressed, I continued seeking companionship with other women, reconnecting with one of my high school sweethearts whom I was able to contact via telephone and letters. These Women not only answered my letters and calls, they gave me great advice, came to visit and assisted my needs. In return I guided them to financial success via stock market and investments and startup businesses.

CHAPTER 2:
Unconditional Conditions

At this time I challenge you all to look beyond your conditional love and be more open minded, learning from your flaws, your mate's flaws, the state of your relationship and your current situation. Seek to benefit in times of adversity, turn your obstacles into opportunities. Things aren't always what they appear to be. Just because a situation takes a turn for the worst, doesn't mean nothing good can come from it, it just takes for us to be open minded and for our love to be unconditional.

How do we determine who we should love unconditionally? My answer will always be "We don't choose who we love, love just happens." It's a growing feeling and emotion which transforms into a devotion and a dedication to someone, but my belief is often one companion loves the other more then they love them. I advise us all to reciprocate our love and take the initiative to be loving, kind, romantic, exciting and fun. If your love isn't reciprocated, then maybe you should make some terms and conditions, and rethink your relationship entirely. Most importantly, you should communicate with your mate about your thoughts, their actions and exactly both of your wants and desires, within your relationship and outside of it.

Maybe you want to discuss boundaries and expectations of one another. Your opinion should matter equally to your mates and so should your decisions. Until your companion start taken the steps to fully reciprocate your love, you should humble yourself and don't be so zealous to profess and show your love. In most relationships there's always a favor for a favor.

Favor for a Favor: It's innate to do a favor for a friend or companion if you're able to. Then there are those people who do favors for every and anyone, and seek nothing in return, but who has time for that? Are you the type to pull over for a hitch hiker and allow them to enter your vehicle? Then give you directions to where they're going, while allowing them to persuade you to go off your path? Only to assure that they make it to their destination safely? (Those who pick up hitch hikers aren't only killed in movies, they often very well die in real life) If you are this concerned about others some people will call you gullible or naive but maybe you're just a very nice person. Though there are very nice people in this world, no one wants to be used, unless they're receiving something in return.

Does your spouse love you more than you love them? Are they showering you with gifts, affection, romantic dates and vacations, but you don't give back anything in return? If you fit this criteria, please be aware that sooner or later, your companion will eventually become tired of doing all the giving. Even if you can't afford to purchase them gifts, you should return the favor by doing kind gestures and showing your appreciation. That is if you would like the attention, gifts, vacations and romantic dates to keep coming. In a prior relationship, my female companion was a full time student attending Brooklyn College. She worked part time, and couldn't afford rent so I paid for her to live in a room inside a three family home in Flatbush Brooklyn. I also clothed and fed her, taking care of her as if she was mine, in which she was. Along with providing her with basic means of day to day living, I showered her with gifts and took her to exciting and entertaining places on the weekends. Though she couldn't afford to repay me, she would cook meals for me daily and perform long, soothing full body massages on me every evening, followed by amazing sexual intercourse then oral sex. After I ejaculated, she would suck my testicles while humming, causing a vibration sensation which would place me in a state of tranquility and sexual gratification. Though I may have spent a few thousand dollars a month on Janice, her seductive, sexual, soothing stimulation was priceless. For those of you that may think that what I've just described is a form of prostitution, then I'll give you another scenario where you can show your appreciation without providing sexual favors in return.

While with my ex-wife, I was having an affair with a woman who was a registered nurse that worked full time at Methodist Hospital and as always, I showered her with gifts, romance and expensive trips. Initially, I didn't tell her that I was married or that I was a drug dealer but by our fourth date, the chemistry between us was so effortless and magical, that I couldn't stand gazing into her eyes while concealing the truth. After an exciting day of horse back riding and jet skiing, we ended the night drinking while walking on Coney Island boardwalk, where I divulged that I was unhappily married. She gazed into my eyes and uttered "I'm disappointed that you're just telling me this but I appreciate you telling me the truth." She then placed her hand against my face, then passionately kissed me.

The following day, she invited me to a karaoke lounge but she didn't sing, she wrote a song dedicated about our relationship titled "I never want us to end" which I enjoyed and for the first time learned that Janice had a voice which can only be described as a gift from above.

Subsequently I received a small package with a red bow wrapped around it, with only a return address labeled Misses. Inside was a DVD. Intrigued! I immediately slid it into my DVD player and pressed play. A blank screen appeared, within seconds, large, red script letters rolled up the screen that read "To my wonderful man, thanks for showing me what life is about. Though I never been in love, I think it best to describe the feelings that I feel for you" followed by several pictures of Janice and I hugging, holding hands, kissing or just out and about enjoying the moment. I realized that over those ten months of dating, we went out often and took a lot of pictures together and though she knew I was married, she wanted these special experiences to continue.

The manufacturing of this DVD couldn't have been more than $50 but the overwhelming feeling that came over me as I watched Janice and I living and enjoying life through this phenomenal art work was priceless and more meaningful then the money I've spent on her over these prior months. The thought that Janice put into this small gift is what counted the most and the fact that she wanted these memories to play out like her dream movie is what made me feel special. To this day, if I hear the song "Have You Ever" recorded by Brandy, I think of Janice and her DVD. Even if you're on a budget, you can be creative when it comes to showing your appreciation for your mate, in small ways or in large but when the sun sets, it's really the thought that counts. Via email reply, how many of you like to be seduced? Pleasured and sexually stimulated until you just can't endure anymore? Now, how many of you return these same sexual pleasures that have been bestowed upon you? When it comes to sex, it would be a false statement to say that we are all created equal but I will say this, with sex, we all need to be creative!

Sexual favors should definitely be returned, you should want to please your mate the same, or even better than how they pleased you. In every relationship, it should be a give and take situation, especially when it comes to sex. Even in the bible it states "Do on to others, as you would want done to you" meaning, if you like to receive oral sex, then you ultimately have to give oral sex. The more you give, the more you shall receive. If you don't know how to perform oral sex, I'll prepare a video designed specifically to teach, yes you guessed it, for both women and men. Email over your information! alltheanswers1000@gmail.com

"If I cook for us, the least you can do is wash the dishes" When your companion invites you over for dinner, are you the type to eat the meal provided, sip some wine or your favorite alcoholic beverage then relax on the couch with your feet up? Without even offering to clear the table or wash the dishes? If so, you should consider offering a hand in the clean up process. Even if you don't want to because your mate will probably say, "No babe, I got this. I'm serving you this evening, just go relax, find something to watch on TV while I clean up". A kind gesture of offering to do the dishes is a sign of appreciation to your companion, for taking the time out and putting the effort into preparing your delicious, intimate dinner. These small offerings are often overlooked and go unasked but these same small offerings, allow your mate to know that their catering hasn't gone unnoticed and that you're willing to put in some effort and help with the clean up since they've done all the preparation.

Another way of expressing that you're grateful for your mates services is cooking and preparing a nice intimate dinner in return but it is essential that you go a bit more above and beyond measures. How about serving them their food in a sexy outfit surrounded by candle lights with their favorite love song playing in the background. Then how about you pull your chair right beside theirs and slowly feed their food to them with some extra affection. While divulging your true feelings for them about your relationship feed them some sexy dessert after dinner. Following dessert start your strip tease, leading to actual stripping which will definitely lead to great sex. For those of you that are in new relationships and don't want to feel like a prostitute, you can fall asleep after you perform your strip dance or not. Most or nearly all men, love a lady in the streets and a freak in the sheets (in the bed), so feeling like a prostitute could actually be a great thing. You can even give yourself a sexy, sex slave name or if you're the aggressor, a sexy dominate name as your alter ego. Though its essential to have at your own disposal a safe word. There are proper bondage tools to utilize when you're in your masochistic mode, so feel free to go shopping at your local novelty store for your chains, whips, gags, leather mask and all other items needed for your sexual pleasures.

There's numerous ways to express your appreciation, though the favor that you return may not be equate, it's the thought that counts. Have you ever awaken early on the weekend but didn't have much to do? Well, this would be the perfect time to do your companions laundry, then fold their clothes, clean their home and maybe reorganize those out of order items that annoy your life like those sneakers, shoes, clothes in their closet. Or how about the items in the cabinet that are carelessly thrown around, just like the food in the refrigerator. Speaking of which, one would really feel good when they open their refrigerator and surprisingly its filled with all their favorite foods, juices, snacks, etc. These small gestures really shows you care because these situations require detail which means that in order to complete the task, you must have been paying attention to their wants, needs, and desires. Details can be as small as restocking your mates favorite dessert, toothpaste, body soap or as big as paying their car insurance, home owners insurance, rent, and paying off their student loan.

Upon wowing your mate with continuous surprises, meeting their parents and family is guaranteed to follow, it is now up to you to decide whether you want the potential in laws as your allies or enemies. Surprising your mate family members with kindness, would do more than just win over your man and have him ready to propose, start a family, and worship the grown you walk on. It will gain you allies with your extended family and if you could win over his mother, you'll have him eating out much more than just the palm of your hands.

The favor of showering your man's mom with attention such as just saying, "Hello" via text messages, phone calls inquiring about her well being is always a bonus. Asking if she needs anything, treating her to get her hair and nails done or taking her shopping, can build an unbreakable bond, where Momma Love will ultimately help her prince realize that you are the one and this sort of favor returned is priceless.

"Keep him romancing by keeping it sexy" In the beginning most men do whatever it takes to get the woman they want. Then overtime it seems like once they have you, they don't have to work as hard anymore. Ladies, this is where I need you to keep them focused on the prize. You do know that you are considered their trophy right? Similar to winning the Super Bowl, championship game, or the world series. See, most athletes win their championship rings then go relax for months on in, until preseason starts back up. In the meantime your goal is to make sure that you're their number one priority. There is no slipping! Your relationship on both parts, should be like a full time career all year round but instead of the strenuous work, you have to think smarter! Not work harder! For starters, instead of asking your man "Do you have any plans for us this weekend?" Notifying him in advance about tickets you purchased on his card, or with his cash to the concert of your choice, headlining your favorite artist will do. If you would like a more intimate setting then reservations for two at your favorite 5 star restaurant, will suffice. Leave no room for him to choose you second, third or fourth for that matter. Besides business, you should be his top priority and every once in a while, allow him time for the "Fellas".

Now ladies, you can't be lacking in your womanly duties either. The best way to keep your man romancing you is by keeping it sexy and showing him that you're all the woman he'll ever need. Please, try your best not to constantly wear those ugly scarfs to bed. If you have no other way of preserving your hair I suggest turn off the lights first then put on your scarf, or wait until he falls asleep. Another thing I suggest is stop getting your hair done in front of him. If possible don't let him catch you slipping, with half of your weave in or having your hair in total disarray. Yes, he should love you regardless but allowing him to see only the finish product keeps him anticipating. Those flowers you receive is not for having your hair undone, what keeps a man fully into you is showing him how sexy you can keep it. Overtime your man sees you at your most vulnerable time, but you want him thinking, "Damn, my lady is bad. I might as well go ahead and put a ring on it" Even if you're just lounging around the house, wear some spandex or boy shorts revealing that sexy tight body of yours, tank tops and belly shirts are also great house wear to preserve your sexy. And when your night is coming to an end, slip into some lingerie (I'll go into more details about lingerie later), when you're going out, throw on your best, form fitting is always a yes, a little revealing but classy I suggest. Remember, he doesn't have to guess.

When out and about for a night cap, or when the opportunity presents itself, seize the moment. Have that quickie in mid-air on your returning flight from Cancun or in the restroom of that 5 star restaurant that you frequent. You can start by sliding your panties off from under your dress, tossing them to your mate prior to your sexual engagement. This single act alone, would stir your mate's mind with provocative, sexual thoughts, often causing an automatic erection.

The more you keep it sexy, the more you'll have your man lusting for you, watching your every move, paying attention to details and wanting to please you. Now that he's eating out the palm of your hands, you literally treat him like a dog, throwing him a treat of something sweet while keeping him in line. First thing first though, you have to train him just like you teach your dog to roll over. If he's driving for the day, stand in front of the passenger door until he opens your door for you, even if it takes for him to sit in the driver seat before he realizes that you're still standing there. When your man pulls into the parking lot, garage, or parking spot at the curb, allow him to exit the vehicle then walk over to the passenger side and open your door. Even if it means watching him walk off towards the movie theater before he realizes that his queen is still sitting in the car, waiting for her door to be opened. Remember, shivery isn't dead unless you kill it.

Subsequently to him learning to open the car door and every other door that you walk through when he's with you, reward him with a strip tease and lap dance in your sexiest lingerie. You may want to consider role playing. How about a sexier superhero as your alter ego! Cat Woman! Super girl! Super Woman? Storm! Even the Sexy wicked witch would do, or if you want to keep it simple, the Sexy School Girl always works for me.

Keeping it sexy doesn't only mean, having one or many desire you by the sex appeal of your dress code. Your sexy can be shown in your attitude, how you talk, tone of your voice, how you respond and react in day to day situations. Your walk, your strut, your waltz with a slight switch, could be sexy. Your sexiness can be shown through your facial expression, your smile, your grin, your laugh, the way you squint your eyes, or lower and raise your eyebrows. Even the way you express how upset you are when you pout your sexy lips and put on your mean face. Exposing that little wrinkle over your nose often causes an unsuspecting erection.

Let's do this, I challenge you to find some quiet time alone, in secret, clothed or in the nude. Find your favorite mirror in your home and examine yourself from head to toe, find the things about you that you feel are sexy and pose from different angles, gazing at yourself, owning your sexiness, becoming one with your sexiness and building confidence in yourself. For the already confident ones I commend you, now apply that same synergy to your wants and needs.

Knowing that you're sexy and being sexy is powerful. Ladies, I want you to work on your sexy, perfect your sexy and illuminate it when the time is right. Master your sexy and you will master the mind of your man and many others that enter your circumference. Once you master the mind of your man, his romance, spontaneous kind acts, foreplay, oral sex, spoiling you with gifts and vacations, will never stop. In fact, you may need some time away with your girls so you can show off your new gifts and brag about how wonderful your man has been treating you.

On the next girl's night out your friends will immediately notice the rock on your finger. So now is the time to decide who you'll have as your brides maid, think long and hard about it because this wedding will be one to die for because as you know, it's until death do you part.

Even after you master your sexy and master the mind of your mate, never allow him to get too comfortable. Living with your spouse, from work, to home, dinner to bath, to bed, often becomes routine and if you're like me, being repetitious is extremely boring. Boring often leads to distraction and arguments, resulting in an inevitable break up or divorce. To avoid the break ups and divorce, don't become so comfortable that your life is routine. If you don't become comfortable, you leave him no room to fall off from his responsibilities, which is making sure that you're happy. Happy spouse keeps a happy house.

In order to prevent your spouse from becoming comfortable means telling them what you want and how you want it, "Babe, let's go to the Beyonce concert at the Barclays Center next weekend", "I thought we were doing dinner at my mother's house" "I'm tired of going over there every week, let's do something different" Ladies, this is a prime example of what you need to do and how you do it.

First, initiate the solution to the problem that may or may not exist and if he gives you a rebuttal or a reason why he can't meet your request, express how you feel which will solve two problems with two lips. He has now realized you're unhappy which should cause him to meet your demands. Inform his mother that his weekends will be spent spending romantic quality time with his wife. Keep in mind that adding entertainment to your schedule, doing the things you both like to do will prohibit him from becoming complacent.

Chapter 3:
Love Yourself First

In order to fully love your spouse you have to love yourself. You love yourself by making yourself happy even if it means altering their decisions and disagreeing with their actions if you are unhappy.

The word LOVE is defined as; strong affection, warm attachment, attraction based on sexual desire, a beloved person, unselfish loyal and benevolent concern for others.

Some of us are looking for love in all the wrong places, others found love and let it go, or still fighting for it not to leave. Then there are those that simply gave up on love all together. Personally love found me, well my wife actually took the initiative to approach me and begin a conversation which was love at first sight specifically pertaining to attraction based on sexual desire, in other words I said to myself I would eat her pussy and fuck her to the sun rise, the warm attachment and loyalty came later.

My reason for defining the word love again is because some of us didn't know what it actually meant. Or we use the word loosely and carelessly without action. Throughout the world the word love is smeared across our televisions as if it has no real significance. Within the last decade talk shows, reality shows, sitcoms, movies, music and video games discredited and disgraced the word love more than ever before.

Study has proven that the number one reason that most people say they love someone then show them the total opposite is because most of us don't know what love is. How can you love someone when you don't even know what love is? We have to first learn what love is, and love ourselves before we can fully love someone else. To love yourself is to know yourself. Now ask yourself "Do I know myself?" Yeah, you know your name, birthdate and social security number I hope, but do you know who you are? What you want? What you need? Most importantly where you're going in life? Have you overcome your childhood fears, and built up emotions? Do you even know how to love?

We all conclude that no one is perfect, we all have flaws and some of our flaws are bigger than others but a part of knowing yourself is knowing and seeking to correct or live with your flaws.

Some flaws we can't get rid of and if you tried to but failed, I give you a huge round of applause because failure can be used as progress. Now that you figured out that you can't rid yourself of some imperfections, lets learn how to deal with them. Either figure out how to use your imperfections as an advantage or cover them up as much as you can, whether they're physically, emotionally, mentally, or financially! Or end up like Aaron Hernandez, a man that seemingly accomplished an American dream of becoming a multi-millionaire NFL player with the New England Patriots but was living with demons as a gay killer who later was convicted of murder and was acquitted on two other murders. Though he was fighting an appeal he hung himself in prison when the world found out that he was gay. Some people hide, bottled up emotions until they uncontrollably erupt at once, this often happens at a time when you're left to deal with it all alone.

Once you've figured out the hard part which is your cons, you can now move on to the easy things in life like your pros, which are the positive things about you. The positives are usually your attributes that you take a liking to or that people often compliment you on throughout life. How you balance your pros and cons determine who you are. Once you know and accept who you are you must learn how to apply your pros and cons to benefit yourself. In the process of living life, before dating and beginning a serious relationship you should know how, when and when not to apply your pros and cons.

Your pros may give off the wrong impression at times. For example, lets say your'e a female with large breast, showing lots of cleavage to go meet your boyfriends parents for the first time may not be a good idea. Image is not everything, but first impression's can leave a long lasting perception. If one of your cons is that you are often over opinionated then while on a first date with someone you would like to see again you may want to keep most opinions to yourself, that is until the third date at least. Once you master your pros and cons the "I like myself," attitude becomes "I love myself." Here's one way of knowing you love yourself, your attitude change from negative to positive.

ATTITUDE: a mental position or feeling with regard to a factor or state, the position of something in relation to something else. Attitude is 100% of everything.

Your attitude alters your altitude, meaning with a bad attitude you limit yourself from all the opportunities in front of you. With a great attitude you can fly high. The sky is unlimited your opportunities are endless. Attitude is in everything you do, from brushing your teeth in the morning to having sex with your mate, to your work performance at the office. When you love yourself your attitude will show in a positive way, frowns now become smiles. You will feel different about the way you view Life in general. Your road rage will cease and the person that brushes up against you on the train wouldn't bother you as much. You are now in transformation from a pessimist to an optimist.

Your close friends and family will take notice to the new you. Your positive energy won't allow you to become easily annoyed by coworkers. You will be able to make each situation more pleasant, you'll have a better outcome from the way you handle events and deal with people. Most grumpy, mean, or people with bad attitudes have issues within themselves that keep them from being happy. Either they don't love themselves enough to make a change in their abnormal behavior or they don't love themselves enough to know that they have a problem. When they do finally encounter a happy moment it's usually short-lived because they are too focused on the negative. I guess it's up to us happy people to bring it to their attention and help them to transform into a positive being. I know what y'all thinking, there are some mean or grumpy people with bad attitudes that's married or in a long-term relationship. In those cases it's usually because of financial gain involved or great sex. Great sex often keeps two or three people together even though they're not happy and some great oral sex can keep someone around even longer.

I know most would like to remain on the topic of sex, but we'll get back to that. At this time I would like to talk to my single people, my single people that love themselves. Are you ready to seek your mate? Meet your mate, and possibly keep your mate? If the answer is yes you have to first find out what is your wants and needs. Do you want a guy/gal that's into sports like you? Do you want a companion that has children, possibly the same age as yours? Would you like someone that does not have any children? For single parents seeking new relationships the dating game is a lot more difficult because you're not only seeking a companion for yourself. You're also looking for someone that will eventually except your child/children and hopefully form a connection with them. Who knows, your new mate may end up being their step mom or step dad. At this moment your focus should be on what you want and what you need.

What's most important in a relationship to you? Money! Are you looking for a wealthy companion? There's nothing wrong with that, most people are. The question remains, "Is someone single and wealthy looking for you?" What do you have to offer besides your beauty? As you may know our looks fade as we age, but money doesn't. On second thought, with money you can have numerous cosmetic surgeries!

I challenge you all to give a good reason why someone rich would choose you as a mate? (alltheanswers1000@gmail.com)

Let's suppose you are a great catch with great qualities, compatible for a wealthy companion, where would you go to find Mr./Ms. Wealthy? Can you tell if someone is rich by their appearance? Certainly not! I'm guessing you would have to do your own research on how to find the rich and single. Maybe one those fortune 500 clubs is a good place to start. It may be a difficult task to find a rich mate that's not famous. How do you enter their circumference? How would you be able to start a conversation? It's not impossible, but you do have to do some investigating and in the process make sure you don't turn into a stalker. Overall, only one percent of the world's population is actually wealthy, but you can think about possibly settling for someone that's just well off. Do you know the difference?

Let's lower the stakes a little, are you willing to accept someone with a good paying job with benefits? Or someone doing fine financially and are good at running their own business? I agree, option 2 is more reasonable. Realistically I believe you're better off trying to find someone that you can become wealthy with rather than finding someone that's already wealthy. Here's why! Besides those that inherit a fortune or win huge amounts of currency from settlements most likely worked hard for their financial success. Which means they're commonly overprotective of the prized possessions. Even if you find one of the "wealthy only club members" you would have to work 10 times harder to prove your love or find yourself kindly placed into the "he/she only wants me for my money category" I'm not saying that it's impossible but the odds are stacked against you.

Finding a companion with a good paying job and benefits is not a bad idea, believe it or not it's very common. One of my all-time favorite clichés goes, "Two heads are better then one" you and your new mate can be considered the two heads. Just think if you meet the ideal candidate but they're not rich as you once wished for but the two of you want to become rich. Then the two of you can put your thinking caps on, and with the right plan get rich together.

Here's a quick scenario, you both have good paying jobs and you both receive your tax returns each year and decide to save your tax returns collectively for two years to invest in your business plan/invention, while building your credit for a business loan. With the right discipline and money managing tools you two can become a power couple. Simply by saving and investing into your multimillion-dollar business plan or invention. "You have to use what you have to get what you want."

I know I'm thinking many steps ahead into the future, let me slow down a bit and get back on track. We will discuss spouse/business planning in another addition of SLR but I hope you got my point. Finding an already rich mate versus possibly building your own multi-million or billion dollar empire with the right companion, tools, and resources, is more likely.

Now that we understand what would most likely be the outcome of seeking others riches, lets move on to a different category most people may want, though few prefer none. Children are such a blessing! They actually keep most people sane after a bad breakup or divorce. Sometimes children are all some have to show for dedicating years of their lives to their ex companion. Children bring joy to our lives, they keep us youthful and smiling but being a single parent new to the dating game can be awkward for some. How do you go about giving this valuable information to your potentially new significant other?

Honesty is always my philosophy, be straight forward and let your potential mate know that you have a child or children. This topic should be brought up within the first few conversations, to allow them to decide whether your situation is one that they're interested in dealing with. After you reveal your prized possessions you should then inquire if they have children of their own and ask the status of their relationship with their children and the co-parent of their children. These answers would shed light on what type of individual they truly are. Often many may continue having sex with their ex-companion though they're not "together" simply for convenience sake.

Then there are those men that try to hide the fact that they even have a child, or several children but eventually if you stay long enough they'll get caught in their own web of deceit. On another side of the spectrum there are those men who don't take care of their children and deny them from birth. You know those dead beats! Not to bash men but I will say that there are many that are selfish and irresponsible when it comes towards their children. Some are so irresponsible that they're leaving their child behind do to irreconcilable differences with their ex. I'm just saying, men we have do better, and for the women that keep their children away from their Dad to be spiteful, you are only hurting the child.

My women, some of y'all are not out of the doghouse yet. There are some of you that make it extremely difficult for your children to have any type of relationship with their father. Creating drama for the father to take the child for the weekend or even visit for that matter. Y'all have to stop using your children as a bargaining tool or as a way to prove that you still have some power over your ex's decision making.

Before we move on, people lets stop airing all of our personal lives on social media. Everything isn't for everybody. Some Women go as far as reading a post their child's father posted on his social media page about an event he's attending on a certain day. She then decides to ruin his plans by bringing the child over on that specific day only to return the next day for pickup just to be spiteful. Let's stop all the drama ladies, you are only creating obstacles for yourselves. I strongly advise that you work on reconciling your situations with your children father's before looking for a new mate.

The best solution to avoid future betrayal is to bring all the possible problems to the forefront. Once it's established that you or your new date have children with their ex, you now have to find out what their relationship is like. That is of course if you're willing to date someone that already have children. Many have already decided that a new candidate with children is a deal breaker. Then there are others that are open minded about finding love with one that previously procreated. Which one are you?

If your'e open to dating people that already have children, you may find out that their relationship consist of day to day communication with their ex. In this type of situation there's a strong possibility that they're occasionally having sex with their ex. These interactions usually last until one or the other finds someone better to replace them. Even with a potential replacement, a quickie here and there may still exist. Research has proven that the common bond of bringing life into this world with someone plays a significant part in anyone's life. At some point or another, most will always have a place in ones heart for that special person.

At this point you may feel that you can break this bond, but is this person even worth the trouble? If you and your new potential lover have a lot in common and you're really into them, I say go for it. Hey you never know! Do keep in mind that you have to work twice as hard to win their heart, that is if their ex is competition and a hard act to follow, but first make sure that the feelings are mutual.

Now that you know what you want in a mate, where do you search for one? A dating app? Let's be real If you live in a city that never sleep like New York, no need for online dating. In my city I can walk to the store and meet a new person of interest.

Let's take sports for example, maybe you're a big sports fan that love football. If you attend some or most of your favorite team games, a football game would be a great place to meet a companion.

While in line at the concession stand if you see an attractive potential, don't be shy approach them. Ask if you can wait in line with them, or if they're behind you wave to them. Grab their attention and signal them to come closer. When they decide to take advantage of the line advancement introduce yourself then tell them why you invited them over. Be totally honest, compliment them on their beauty, ask if they're attending the game with a significant other then further inquire whether or not they are single.

TOUCHDOWN! They are single and attracted to you as well. Talk about the game, ask what team they're rooting for? That is if they're not wearing their favorite team apparel. Even if they're rooting for the opposite team you already have a lot in common. Find out what they're ordering, comment on what you like and maybe even offer to treat. Before you part ways be sure to ask, "Is it possible for us to exchange numbers?" After a great spontaneous conversation the answer would most likely be "sure".

A fun filled environment is one of the best places to start a conversation. I actually met my wife in a similar situation. We both were attending a mutual friend's (fight party) Shane Mosley vs. Oscar De La Hoya. I sat down next to her observing her from head to heel, inhaling her enticing fragrance, listening to her sexy Latin accent as she spoke loudly to her female associates. Initially I tuned in to the fight to become abreast of who was winning, $10,000 was on the line. Soon after she accidentally picked up my cup of Hennessy on the rocks mistaking it for her long island ice-tea. "EEEEEL, how do you drink that! It's disgusting" she uttered. I then took a sip of her long island ice-tea and we conversed through the evening while rooting for opposite opponents. It was intriguing anticipating the outcome when surprisingly she waited outside the restroom for me leading to an exchange of phone numbers. Our subsequent dates lead to sex, excitement, pleasure, companionship, loyalty, love, fun, passion, bliss, then marriage. Initially we were physically attracted to one another in an entertaining drama free setting where we were able to share laughter and indulge in conversation. Perfect setting for sparks to fly which we now would call love at first sight.

Of course there's more in debt details that I'll talk about some other time about our relationship! Point being is that from the very beginning we already had something in common which was boxing as one form of entertainment.

Not into sports? Maybe you like the line of work that you're in? How about that co-worker you had your eye on ever since you started working there? Though the office is not always fun, things can get interesting every now and then especially during lunch breaks and those holiday parties.

Actually the workplace is a great place to find love, you can find out all the right or wrong things you need to know about that individual before becoming fully acquainted with them. The best part about dating someone at the work place is being secretive, well at least initially but sooner than later everyone finds out. Another good thing about the workplace is time. Timing plays a major role where you don't have to rush anything. So stop procrastinating and inquire whether or not they're involved, if not you can be very creative in this type of situation. I advise that you send them an anonymous email being flirtatious, fill their heads with compliments and see if they begin to smile more throughout the course of the day.

Remain anonymous for a few days while you ask them questions that you need to know before revealing yourself. If the individual seems flattered and respond promptly, that means they're into it and they've taken the bait. Go for it, keep them guessing a few more days while you pick their brain. When you decide that you're ready to reveal yourself give them a brief description of who you are without going into detail. See if they can guess who you are. The suspense alone is sexy, the person becomes intrigued and begin to wonder who it is. That same wondering becomes a fantasy, if you say all the right things.

Ladies this means you too, don't be shy. Most men love aggressive women believe it or not, not too aggressive though. Besides if he's a great catch don't you think all the other women in the workplace have their eyes on him too? These are just a couple examples on how to pursue your ideal mate, just keep in mind that you have to know what you want before you pursue it.

Another scenario could be that you've just met someone that you're physically attracted to and you cant decide where to go on your first date. It may sound typical but restaurants are a great place for first dates. Why? Restaurants are open to the public, just incase you want to end the date early without incident. Though the setting should be intimate it's just right to see how attracted to them you are and not just their looks. This setting gives you the perfect opportunity to ask as many questions as possible, check for table manners, proper etiquette, (if you're that type) expensive or inexpensive taste, the type of vehicle they may or may not have, their style of dress on an average night out, how often their phone rings and how many calls go unanswered. Do they pay cash/credit or even offer to pay at all, hey some women will even offer to pay for everything if they're really enjoying themselves.

What does all of this mean? A lot of you can find out if the person isn't right on the very first date. At times it's good to disregard the physical attraction momentarily to focus on their attitude toward yourself and others? Are they courteous to the waitress/waiter? Do they give off a positive vibe? Initially how did they greet you? Did they compliment you? Is there anything that you feel the urge to compliment them on? Are you close enough to smell their fragrance or perhaps their breath?

Another important factor is religion. What religion are you? Or are you atheist? Lets say you meet someone that you're physically attracted to but find out they believe in a different religion or have different beliefs in religion as a whole! Do you want to challenge yourself and try to convert them into believing what you believe? Or do you want to move on and give up on those possibilities?

Some would take the challenge. Would you be open to converting? Conversion of religion is a challenge in itself, you would have to recondition someone's whole way of thinking including their practices, faith and even rituals that they may have done year after year. New beliefs are difficult to get accustom to because you have to condition your mind into thinking whole heartedly that this new information is true facts and that everything you've learned in the past is a lie or has been altered. As an adult it's even harder to take on new beliefs because you've been thinking this way thus far. How do you convert someone from their old beliefs into practicing a new religion? I'm guessing you would preach and practice your beliefs and try to convince them that what you tell them and show them is the truth. Many men have become Muslim because their religious practices allows them to have seven wives but only if they can provide for all seven wives and treat all seven wives equally. Sounds like fun doesn't it! Most other religions believe in one marriage, having one spouse. Are you a one spouse type of person?

Personally my wife and I believe in Christianity which made our relationship so much easier. Though we're far from Saints we try to live a carefree, truthful, sex filled, fun and exciting life. I believe we were meant to be. Ladies when you catch me looking I'm just window shopping for some possible fun for me and my wife! My wife and I share a lot of the same goals and we have a tremendous amount in common. To this day I believe that she's heaven sent!

Overall religion is a difficult subject to touch base on do to all the different aspects stemming from different beliefs. Would you consider converting religions for love? How does a couple progress with different religious beliefs? Which religion would the parents teach their children? These are just a few of the many questions which will arise but ultimately you would have to make the final decision when the time is right.

Another important factor is sex. Are you willing to guide this person on how to please you if he/she could not fulfill your desires? Before we get into sex let's get into their mind. At that very first date you want to find out all you can about this individual, no filters. Don't worry about them thinking that you're too aggressive by asking serious questions, because we have no time to waste on someone you already know won't work.

Your questions should mainly be about things that are important to you, in this case I'll use topics I already spoke about like money, children, and religion. If money is your top priority then your first question should be about money. No, no, no, not "how much money do you make?" that would make your intensions too obvious. Instead you should ask, "What's a typical work day like for you?" Next you should ask, "For how long?" This answer will give you an idea of how far away from starting salary they are or how long they've been in business for themselves. Your following question should be "What do you do on your spare time?" This question will answer a whole lot of questions without the need to ask them. From side business ventures to second jobs to inventions and maybe even stock trading, or not. If their spare time doesn't consist of generating revenue then you can estimate their income based on their day job. Their main business venture will help you further decide the potential of this person being that special one. That is of course if obtaining money is your most important priority.

One of your next questions should be, "Do you have any children?" A yes or no would be suffice. Based on this reply your concerns about being with someone who have children will be answered. If the answer is yes then your next question should be, "How old?" followed by, "Are you still involved with your child parent? Those two answers combined will inform you on how long they've been intimate with their child/children's parent without actually asking the question.

Are you still involved? The answer is usually no even though 7 out of 10 still are. Regardless of all these different answers given, you have to take the initiative in doing your own research. Now that you've picked their brain and most of the answers are to your liking it's time to set up a second date but until then you should take a peak at their social media pages.

First thing you want to check when you locate their social media pages is their relationship status. You would want it to read single but if not scrutinize their pics to see who they're hugged up taking selfies with, they still might be involved or even married. A post that reads "Married" is a definite red flag especially if they have the alleged ex as a "friend" and their status reads married as well but they're tagging each other in pics and constantly leaving comments. "Personally I would lose all contact with them, they're too messy." Really there's no explanation for having a status as married if you're really not or going through a "divorce" which usually takes what seems like forever. Most of you wishful thinkers know exactly what I mean!

If your person of interest status reads "In a relationship" It's not a definite "No go" it just means you have a lot more questions that need to be answered. When the opportunity presents itself you want to ask specific questions on your next date. You don't want to question the social media content over the phone. Ask them in person, you want to look them in their eyes and see the priceless expression on their face, making them aware that yes, you do research on who your potential mate may be. If the person finds it offensive that you've been prying then that's their problem. Be sure to ask about that individual that they've been posting pics with.

If the status reads single that's always a plus but they're not clear just yet, check their background information to make sure that it adds up with what they told you. Read their post and comments, trust me you'll be surprised what you find out about someone by reading their social media pages.

There's a huge difference between stalking and researching. By inquiring whether or not someone works where they say they do is simple homework one must do before letting a new person into their life. Go to their alleged work place, wait outside in your car and check if they come out around the time they say they get off. If you're too busy then show a close friend their picture and have them go check. If someone lied about their workplace that's a big deal, that's not at all considered a little white lie. More like a huge lie, where someone work's state a lot about them, our workplace is usually where we spend most of our time. Some of us even bring our work home with us so yes, a persons job description is extremely important. If an individual lied about where they work you have to think, what else did they lie about? Is this individual even worth more of your time?

Come to find out they've been telling the truth all along. If money is highly significant along with a great orgasm then what you want to do next is google their starting salary. I challenge you to calculate their starting salary with at least a one dollar raise per year, multiplied by how many years they've been on the job to establish what their bank account is like. Sounds like too much work? Well, being that you may be sharing your bed with this person you need to know their income because you should be aware that unprotected sex leads to pregnancy. These common situations sometimes lead to unwanted, and expensive children.

All the information you've received thus far has been accurate, you're satisfied with the answers you've obtained, so what's the next step? Let's switch things up a bit before the next date. If you've been consistently calling your potential companion early evenings you should now start calling around 10 p.m. Even if they call you early in the day, a couple of "I'm a call you back later!" wouldn't hurt. postpone the conversation until the evening. You need to find out who your potential mate is with right before bedtime. If you call and receive no answer this could be a sign that they secretly live with someone in which they want to remain anonymous. Give them an hour, if they don't call back call again. Remember this isn't stalking it's called research. You want to know who they're going to bed with before you decide to go to bed with them. They didn't call you back yet? Don't stress it, wait until they call you the next day, postpone a couple of their calls, then call them back at 11 p.m.

11 p.m. is the average bedtime for any working class person. Even if you're sleeping and the phone awakens you, wouldn't you at least pick up for someone you're interested in even if it's just to tell them, "I'm sleeping, I'll call you in the morning." At least I would, that is if I have plans to

keep this person in my near future. On the second day you try reaching out at 10 p.m. and still no answer chances are they're living with a significant other or they conveniently don't want to talk to you in front of their "acquaintance". Well, there is still a small chance that they turn their ringer off before bed or they just wasn't thrilled about the fact that you've awakened them from their sleep for the second time in a row. Now the question is, did they specifically tell you "Don't call me after ten p.m. because I'll be sleep."

On the third day when they call please feel free to pick up because this individual have some explaining to do. If the excuse is good enough do proceed with caution. If it wasn't, then you know what to do! Assume what they're doing. Are you willing to move forward with a new potential mate even if they are already dating someone? Maybe you can tame them into whatever you want them to be? Or are you willing to share your mate with someone else?

What if they passed the phone test and picked up at 10 p.m.? Or had a good enough reason why they didn't and on the 3rd date y'all had a blast. Y'all kissed goodnight and you've been turned on ever since, is it time to let go and take it to that sexual level? If you made it to the 3rd date without fulfilling your sexual desires then you're better then most. I'm just being honest for you "Saints" out there. 95% of Americans practice premarital sex as well as test drive their vehicle before purchasing it. 60% of us try on our clothes at the store before buying them so I'm guessing we do the same with our companions. We're only human, and I know that it's extremely difficult to date someone for a period of time and not become sexually aroused and sexually inquisitive at some point.

Chapter 4: That Sex Talk

"SEX" The word as defined in the new edition Mirriam Webster Dictionary describes sex as; either of two major forms that occur in many living things and are designated male or female according to their role in reproduction; also the qualities by which these sexes are differentiated and which directly or indirectly function in reproduction involving two parents. SEXUAL ACTIVITY or BEHAVIOR; ALSO SEXUAL INTERCOURSE!

In the United States 8 out of 10 marriages end in divorce do to adultery. Across the nation, sexual immorality has almost become the norm. Why is that? Why is most people so fascinated with sex? Is it the pleasure one receive from it? Is it just the lustful desire for it? Or is it the fact that we as human beings need sex to survive? These topics and many more are always open for discussion so we can better understand sex, love, and how to preserve our relationships, whether it's an open relationship, newly found infidelity, monogamous or a love triangle.

The act of sexual pleasure when performed properly can bring forth such an overwhelming orgasmic sensation throughout the body that once one experiences this, he/she may become addicted. The first orgasm that most of us share is usually the best one, yet many of us search endlessly to create that feeling perpetually, but often fail to the lack of consistency with their mate or finding that special person that knows your anatomy well enough to satisfy you at every opportunity. Let's not get discouraged because the perfect orgasm can be a hard act to follow.

Knowing your body, knowing what your body desires and practicing pleasuring your sexual needs with your companion can bring about this perfect orgasm that one seek. We all do know that practice makes perfect right! Just like in any sport you have the professionals then the amateurs who wish they were professional. Which one are you? We have to look at sex like a competitive sport, and you want to be the champion, and all champions consistently practiced before they became great at what they do. Are you great at what you do in the bedroom, or in the office, pool, vehicle and any other place you desire.

For those that have never experienced an orgasm I feel empathy for you. Just kidding, maybe you're a virgin patiently waiting for that special someone. Maybe you're holding back and prohibiting your mind and body from enjoying the pleasures collectively. Your body may be being stimulated but if your mind is elsewhere then that can be a major issue or vice versa. Possibly your mate doesn't know how to stimulate you, or stimulate you long enough to reach the climax that you've been longing for. You may just need them to bring out your sexual side, that sexy alter ego that has yet to come out. Or are you one of those people who's just not a sexual being, do you just like the thought of an orgasm but aren't fond of some of the sexual acts itself?

There's several different reasons why some have yet to experience an orgasm, maybe later I'll share some tips on how you too can experience an orgasm yourself. As for me, I continue to enjoy sexual stimulations, just about every chance I get alone with my wife! Sometimes even when we're not alone! Yes, she share this satisfaction also or so she act as if she does very well. Yes, I'm fully aware of you ladies often faking orgasms, but I'm a pleasure seeker for the both of us, I don't stop until you beg me too and if you're faking it's most likely that you cant keep up and want me to stop prematurely!

Some women aren't truthful about the fact that their mate doesn't satisfy them sexually, simply because they don't know how to tell them. In most cases they just don't want to hurt their feelings. Quite often the unpleased companion learns how to find their pleasures else where with sex toys, masturbation or having an affair. For those ladies that have faked orgasms in the past and continue to do so please send me an email, I'm intrigued to know the details. Maybe before this book is complete I'll review my survey and add some answers to "Why Most Women Fake Orgasms" (alltheanswers1000@gmail.com)

Did you know that sex is a great form of exercise? Especially when it's being performed in certain positions. Sex is great for the heart, mind, body and soul. Sex is a desire in life that most seek second to money or even before money. Great sex is addictive, and for many it becomes their drug of choice. I'm guessing sex is the reason why some risk their marriage and disregard their family name like Kevin Heart, when he was caught on video cheating on his wife Eniko Parrish. Many even go to the length that can cost them imprisonment to fulfill their sexual desires by paying for prostitute's who we all know is known to carry a high rate of std's and even deadly ones like AIDS. Then there are those that risk there jobs along with everything else!

Over the last decade there have been a wide spread of school personnel being accused of having sex with underage students. Though this is a whole other topic in itself, these types of situations are becoming less shocking every time we hear about them even when it comes to our politicians. From Bill Clinton who was the 42nd President of the United States scrutinized for his adulterous acts to the 54th governor of New York Mr. Spitzer's sex scandal with prostitutes. Even secret service agents working for Obama in Brazil was accused of having sex with Brazilian prostitutes while on the job. Sex scandals with politicians is becoming the norm. Even politician's to people of importance need sexual pleasure too! The sex industry is big business from adult video's to dildo's to hotlines, sex groups, sex therapy, etc. Even most celebrities can't get enough of sex, some music videos are looking more and more like soft porn which leaves an impression that seems to say, "You need to be having sex right now" and If you let Rihanna tell it, "Sex with me is so amazing." Some of which may be true. In fact a sex tape with R&B singer RayJ turned Kim Kardashian into a house hold name. Now the world watches her sexy steps every step of the way. Over all I strongly suggest that if your objective is to have good sex, do it right and with someone worth sharing yourself with.

Why do you have sex? Most would answer, "Because it feels good." Others would say, "To cum or have an orgasm." Cum by the way is defined as an abbreviation for the word cumulative. Cumulative is defined as increasing in force or value by successive additions. I just figured that was a word many would want to know for the next time you ask your mate, "Did you cum?" or "Do I have cum on my face, or in my hair?"

If most people have sex for the pleasurable feeling that leads to climaxing, shouldn't we all want to share that feeling with someone we love or at least like a lot? Do we depreciate sex each time we indulge in sexual activities with someone we could careless about? I'm guessing only those of us with self-morals and values would even think of the value that sex holds. For those of us who's only into pleasure at any cost, I'm not judging but maybe it's time to learn some self-control which takes discipline of the mind and body. Or maybe not! If you're not at that place in life as of yet then continue to do what makes you happy.

Are you disciplined? Do you use self-control? Or do you have sex whenever, wherever with whoever at any given moment? For some it's only when intoxicated? Whether we realize it or not having random sex places lives at risk, remember condoms break. Not to scare anyone but it's proven facts that there are life defeating diseases out there. Lets all be responsible and get tested. For the record, sex is far more bliss when you share it with someone you love, trust, and are aware of their health status. I'm simply raising this thought provoking topic to help you think about your sexual lifestyle and ask yourself "Is this what I want?" If not, then step your sex game up by elevating your sexual standards. I ask that you continue to journey with me in seeking that right person to enjoy exciting, stimulating, long lasting, fulfilling, romantic, vigorous, pleasurable sex with.

Call me old school but shivery is alive and love is in the air, it's right there for you to catch it before life passes you by but only if you want it.

Ladies and Gentlemen you have to stop and ask yourself, "Am I ready to share my temple with this person of interest?" "Do they deserve me?" and "What does this person have to offer after the fact?" Or you can just enjoy the moment and remove all boundaries, have sex and have sex again! Once these questions are answered and you think this person deserves to share your bed, will you be ashamed if anyone finds out. In today's society it continues to be a double standard of women being called derogatory names for having sex on the first date or with different men as she shop around. When men do the same thing they're actually applauded by their fellow comrades. I understand the slut walk with all do respect to Amber Rose but let's face it, some stereotypes will never change. Just make sure you protect yourself. Allow me to reiterate that spontaneous moments can lead to unwanted pregnancies and much more.

The reason I chose to touch base on this point before I move to the next is because most men really wouldn't wait until the third and forth date. If that sexual opportunity presents itself, most men would be ready to perform on demand. The main difference between men being more, or as promiscuous as women is the fact that men don't get pregnant, not physically at least. For example, a large amount of the deadbeat Dad's that you see appear on the hit show "Paternity Court" moved out of their neighborhood and abandoned their responsibilities. Leaving their pregnant partner stuck with the burden of raising a child by themselves.

Is she a hoe or a slut because she's shopping around for Mr. Right and in the process making a few bad decisions by having sex with Mr. Wrong? Not necessarily, but in today's society, we allow these situations to occur by not providing the proper care and guidance to our youth who don't know what love is. In the course of our young ladies searching for love they accept these guy's whom themselves were misguided and lacking the knowledge of love and responsibly from many different angles. Can we just disregard a contributing factor of why we have this double standard? For those of you that don't mind being called a slut you should just own who you are and maybe go join Amber Rose's "Slut Walk". We all should respect people for who they are. Keep an open mind that to my knowledge there is no school that teaches a curriculum on sex, love and relationships! If there is please inform me! (alltheanswers1000@gmail.com)

In an immaculate world you're sexually frustrated and ready to give yourself to this special individual. Assuming the feelings are mutual, you want to prepare yourself physically, emotionally and mentally. First you research online your closest medical center that provides walk in HIV and STD testing. Once you have your location both of you should take half a day off from work or your Entrepreneurship, for a walk in or scheduled appointment for testing. Trust me this will be one of the most fulfilling dates you will ever go on. This is the date of all dates that will determine your bill of health. While at the clinic or doctors office you should collect the free booklets and read up on the many symptoms of different STD's while you wait. Doing so will educate the both of you, and with knowledge you will enhance the trust and respect level for one another.

Approaching a life changing encounter like having sex we all need to be responsible first for our own health, to assure a long-lasting healthy life, secondly for your mate. Lastly I shall reiterate, to prevent an unwanted pregnancy and std's. This may sound like a bit much but actually it's not. If everyone was to start practicing this habit at the start of their relationship, There will be a drastic drop in death caused by AIDS, less abortions, less single parents and certainly less sexually transmitted diseases.

The test results are in, you and your date are both negative for all std's. Should you now have unprotected sex? Of course not, you should continue to protect yourself at all times just like the referee informs both Boxers before the boxing match. At least until you whole heartedly know that your mate is only sexual with you, or until you and your companion decide you want to bare a child hopefully after marriage. Marriage? There I am getting ahead of myself again, this is a world with no boundaries or order, who needs marriage? Do you want to live free without boundaries? Or do you think it is possible for you to become monogamous?

You are both disease free and you feel that this individual is worth exploring sexually. One of the biggest decisions in your life such as sex with a new partner should be special and well planned. Do your mate live alone? If so choose who's place is more comfortable for the both of you. Yes, this should be a discussion, at some point especially if the two of you don't live alone. Hotels and motels usually work but can become costly. Another suggestion is, ask if your roommate or relatives can give you some alone time for a few hours with your mate.

Set the scenery with lit candles and rose peddles. I shall state for the record many men admit that they feel a bit romantic under candle lights Why not treat your mate to a bubble bath, with candle lights and rose peddles. No, it's not too soon for this! Allow them to relax about ten minutes alone to think about what they want to do to you, and also you're making sure that their clean enough to eat off.

Join them, lather the soap slowly onto your bath sponge or wash cloth. While bathing them continue to sneak preview the whole package. If they're acting shy they just haven't got use to being in the nude around you yet. Some people are self-conscious about their nudity. Let them relax alone a few more moments, while they relax go through their phone, check text messages and call list to see how often and for how long they correspond with selected individuals. Remember the names of those frequently contacted to later question the suspicious text and calls.

Which one of y'all are really doing this? Good! Don't forget to keep me posted with the details.

Return with their robe or towel sprinkled with your favorite fragrance. This way just in case they're returning home to that secret lover they'll have some questions to answer about why they smell like they've been with someone else.

As far as the actual details pertaining to the act of how to perform this sexual encounter, well I cant help you with that at the moment. I tell you what, the next explicit video I make I'll share some of my secrets on sexual pleasures. I can show it better then I can tell it.

Well, how was it? Did this person fulfill your every desire? Did you have an orgasm? Was it your dream cum true? I didn't think it would be either. The first few sexual encounters with a new mate is sometimes awkward. They are so highly anticipated that it ends earlier then expected. The male species sometimes get so excited that they climax prematurely before or during sex. Females are often disappointed the first few time they share their treasure box with their new partner, leaving them dissatisfied, sexually frustrated and prepared to gossip in details to their Friends.

Men are often bashed as "One Minute Man" or that the size of their penis isn't as large as expected. The first time around is not always good but once both parties learn the others anatomy, wants, and needs things usually change for the better. Most Females thrive for more romance and sexual satisfaction while the majority of males seek instant gratification, which almost always leads to them only pleasing themselves. An immediate ejaculation usually occur the first few times because the male over excites and over exhaust himself rather quickly. If males work on more patience, there will be an increase in satisfied women opposed to the dissatisfied female who may now view sex as overrated.

Sex is only overrated to those who are not enjoying it the way they should, who's to blame for these results or what is the blame for these results? There are so many different possibilities! Maybe the female didn't perform well either? She could have put forth a little more effort rather then lay there silently. Perhaps she wasn't in the mood? She was not mentally and physically stimulated. She needed more foreplay before actual sexual intercourse? Maybe her vagina was irritated do to the lack of lubrication.

These are all reasons why communication is the key to all healthy, fun, sex filled, romantic relationships. How can these problems be fixed if your mate doesn't know that there's a problem at all? We need to speak up when there's an issue so that the issue may be resolved. You know the saying, "It's not what you do, but how you do it."

If the first few sexual encounters was terrible, do you give up and stop calling? No, not if you like everything else about this individual. Open up a little and be honest, straight forward to the point. On your next date bring up the topic of sex, ask did they enjoy their previous sexual encounter with you. Let them answer and ask what they liked, or disliked. Most likely they'll answer then return the question. Fill free to speak your mind, first state the things that you did like. Once you have them smiling and feeling comfortable you then add the but, followed by the things you didn't like.

Don't stop there, this is when you add some of your fantasies explaining what you really want. Not the fantasy that you have hidden in your mind that's waiting to be unleashed, no not the wildest one. The basic fantasy of that perfect sexual stimulation that you desire, add the details that you truly want. Yes, its true open mouths get fed faster and a closed mouth won't get you what you want in bed. This conversation can also be a great time to ask about the text messages, that you were inquiring about. Also question, the pictures with that same person of interest, the missed calls by that same individual and everything else that you dislike about the relationship.

This is the start of a new beginning I would say, this conversation marks the time where you both want to clarify where things are going and what demands you need to be met. Yes, I said demands. Everything is on the table, chips are down, they are either going to cash out with just those few sexual encounters or work with you. I guess now you get to talk bad about them at the workplace or wish that you never had met them at that concession stand. Or they're going to take heed to what you are saying because they don't want to lose you. That is if you're on your job, handling the part that you're responsible for which is giving your happiness.

No one is perfect we all need a little polishing here and there, some more than others.

When we are able to fix the problem before our mate have to bring it to our attention then we present ourselves to be flawless. Soon neither one of you will have anything to complain about but these type of actions takes time and discipline.

Before the next date check the social network page or pages of your partner's Instagram, Twitter, Facebook, Snapchat, etc. Do those pictures remain posted with your mate and that person of interest? If so, don't be disappointed, go out on your next date regardless and enjoy yourself. This time when you greet them, inhale deeply. Is that the same cigarette stench that you previously forgot to inquire about? Then ask, do you smoke? If the answer is yes this is good and bad, bad because smoking leads to several long term health issues, typically cancer to be exact. It's also bad because you should have picked that question in the first date. Your mate may have been too embarrassed to tell you at first because of the health-conscious society that we live in. Using all five senses you can find out just about everything. We need to be aware of all things surrounding your companion, especially aromas. A fragrance can open your mind to a lot of things that would have gone unnoticed if it hadn't been for this particular sense of smell.

The strong scent of alcohol on ones breath at the time of your first greeting can mean that this person needs alcohol to function. Often this need is do to a lack of confidence. People with self-esteem issues usually use alcohol to cover up the reality that their state of mind is in. Maybe they're an alcoholic? Or just this one evening they presumed heavily intoxicated.

Marijuana smoking is also a habit some people pickup to mask their inner issues. I'm not passing judgement! I'm just speaking from my own personal issues that I've experienced in the past when I was intoxicated all day everyday. In most instances for someone to be high and drunk means they have found a way to escape reality, but what they're escaping is the bigger issue. Please do inquire within.

Are these habits, issues you can deal with? Then give it a try, hey you may want to indulge. Or if not ask them if it is possible that they slow down or refrain from use when you're around and before you meet. See if they listen, give them a chance, maybe they're willing to cut out these bad habits not only because it's hazardous to ones health but also because you're not fond of it.

If these are habits that you indulge in yourself then perfect, you've met your match. For your future's sake you should try to cut down on all things that distort the mind and slowly eradicate the body. I should mention that certain type of habits open the gateway to many other drugs. The good that may come from all of this is that you may actually change this person's life for the better. This individual might be so into you that they drop their bad habits completely to please you. You have now saved a life.

Attend counseling with them if needed, encourage them to take on new healthy habits. I did mention earlier that sex can be a good exercise. Another good thing that did arise from this situation is that you were able to notice early on and think consciously about continuing the relationship with these known facts. Or calling it quits before giving it your all.

After this night out on the town go to their place, yes insist regardless of the excuse. You want to know how they're living day to day. Ask for a quick tour around the house, apartment, mansion, condo, or basement for that matter. When they finally agree, pay attention to details, like pictures hanging on the wall. Look closely at pictures hanging on the wall or the lack of. When I use to cheat and bring women over to a place I shared with my ex, I would hide me and wifey pics. Look closely at those pictures, see if you happen to come across that same individual from their social media page. If you spot them, then you might just have a problem on your hands. Please feel free to inquire!

Suppose you see a few pictures hanging around and your mate isn't in any of them at all?

Then you should ask questions like, "Are you sure this is your place?" Most guys that still live at their parent's home in their late twenties and older are often too embarrassed to admit it. They most likely would lie about where they live and may take a new companion to a friend or relatives home pretending that this is their place of residents.

Some men and women are so disrespectful that they bring a new date to the dwelling that they share with a companion. Their mate may work two jobs, work nights, or frequently travel on business. This scenario is similar to what happened to Angela Simmons with her baby daddy Sutton Tennyson who brought over the side chick to their home. Sad isn't it, but these are some of the selfish things we do at times to satisfy our sexual appetite. These types of situations almost always end up bad, that's why it's important to look for early signs and ask lots of questions. Not only do you ask questions, you do more research then ask more questions. That's how I always got caught! "Speaking of questions," Where are those missing picture frames that belong in those empty spaces? Chances are those pictures are the pictures of your partner with their real mate. You may be the side chick or side dude.

Check online for a marriage certificate in their name, or maybe they're divorced. Ask questions about their ex, ask why they broke up. If you have any spare time try to find their ex acquaintance on a social network and inquire. Some of the answers you get may be lies, but at least you get to find out what type of company your ex used to keep. Compare the answers from the two then determine who's answers are more believable, your partner's or their ex's. If your mate becomes aware that you contacted their ex and seems to have a problem with it, your reply should be, "I'm just doing my own evaluation to find out the truth, if everything you're saying is true then you have nothing to worry about."

It cost $29.95 for a criminal background check online, it wouldn't be a bad investment either. You'll be surprised how many women have felony convictions from drug trafficking. Yes, drug trafficking! I said it and I'll say it again. "Drug Trafficking," Plenty of beautiful women drive drugs across state lines every day for the love of fast money. Most women are good at it too. Women often talk their way out of speeding tickets by flirting with the officer, showing a little cleavage, and saying all the right things. Women are typically inconspicuous in this line of work mainly because they don't appear to have kilo's of drugs in their trunk. Women are more commonly used for drug trafficking then men. Most women have a cool calm collective aura about them when faced with situations that threatens their freedom. Many of Women throughout the United States and beyond have come across at least one bad guy in their lives who may or may not have corrupted their minds. Some have turned them on to a life of crime, from doing check frauds, credit card scams, prostitution to becoming a getaway driver in a bank heist.

Don't be surprised by the staggering number of women who often get away with murder, literally. Have you ever seen the series on t.v. titled "Deadly Women" Sounds sexy doesn't it? Do those type of women turn you on? I actually do find them intriguing. Before I lose my training of thought, let me continue with criminal background checks online for roughly $29.95. Simply google search the words criminal background check and hundreds of websites will appear. Everyone has a past, what's your's? Is this guy you're dating a convicted rapist? Like Nicki Minaj's husband Kenneth Petty? Or is he a convicted child molester like Nicki Minaj's brother Jelani Maraj?

Is he a stalker? Or just a harmless daytime penis flasher? Hey you never know! One thing I do know is that if your new mate does have a felony conviction you want to question it right away, ask in full details "What happened?" Then maybe you should ask to see the letter of deposition. This document would explain in full detail what really occurred. Or you could just let it slide, and disregard his past.

So you're at your partner's place, everything seem to be in order then suddenly seduction begins. Gently touching and kissing all the right places but in the back of your mind you want to know why they haven't deleted those pictures of interest of their ex, old fling or sex toy? Allow them to become aroused, then pop the question. "Why didn't you delete those pictures yet?" "They might reply, "It slipped my mind" or "I've been busy, I haven't even been on my page." Now it's time for the test, your rebuttal, "Why don't you delete it now?" Depending on this answer and reaction, predicts how this night should end.

"There's no need to delete them, they're just pictures." This answer solidifies that they're still holding on to something, this could be where they're using all their romance and sex acts that they're failing to perform on you. Your reply should be in the nature of, "I think you need to delete those pictures today if you plan on becoming an item." This response is straight to the point, you are now clarifying their intentions with you if they were not yet clear.

Based on the answer to the last question you should proceed accordingly. If they answer, "I'm not ready for a relationship like I thought I was," then you have to decide how you're going to make your exit, quick and harsh? Of course not, let them know that at this time in your life you're looking for a more meaningful relationship. If they're not looking for the same then ask that they stop calling you until they become like minded. No harm no file. "NEXT"

Another option is excepting their current mindset and challenge yourself to change their way of thinking. Can you become second choice in a relationship for a possible long term win? The fact remains that it is extremely difficult to change behaviors and the way people think, especially when they're already complacent.

If the response is complying to your request this means that this individual has potential to take it to the exclusive level. Accompany them to the computer or smart phone, maybe even remember their password, watch as they delete the pictures then reward them with a passionate kiss. Now submit to their sexual advances. Open up a little, don't allow them to do all the work but don't give them too much just yet.

How was it? Did you use protection? Not as bad as the last time? Did you at least climax? If the sex is worst then the last time then I'm afraid you have more of a problem then you thought. Great sex is important in a relationship for many different reasons! The question now remains, is your sex life going to get better or worst? How do you feel about guiding your mate to help them understand what you need? If telling them what you want didn't work, are you willing to show them? This sexual challenge is always interesting, you will find out a lot about your mate and be able to finally determine is this person right for you?

Chapter 5: Sexual Tour Guide

Set the romantic stage for your foreplay. Make sure the candles are lit and the massage oil is close by. You are the director of your movie set, as well as the Actor and screenplay writer. You are in total control take your time, set the mood, and slowly whisper to your mate your every desire. While using all available body parts guide them on how to please you. Open up a little more, the power is in your hands, instruct your partner on how to pleasure you. Direct your mate while physically instructing them what to do…………

Is it working? Maybe a date to the closest novelty store would add some spice to their taste. No, don't act shy! You should try something new! Though sex is very important in a relationship not many of us try new things like a trip to the sex shop in search of the right lubricants, sex toys, role playing outfits and a ton of other assorted novelties. Wait a minute, does this person deserves these new endeavors? Only you can decide when the time is right to take your sex life to the next level. When the time is right, buy a few novelty items to start with and watch how things improve. Save the oral sex for a later date, you'll have plenty more time to get to that. Don't spoil them just yet but of course if their ready to perform on you, just lay back and allow them to explore.

Pleasure should be better in the bedroom by now. If not I would personally give up but that's just me. Or has the sex improved? The two of you are seeing each other more frequently and things are really looking up. Is this person the one? Only time will tell!

Is your new sex filled relationship affecting your business or day job? Are you failing your college courses? Are you getting lower grades then usual? If so, it's time to evaluate your short term goals and possibly alter your long term goals. I bet you never realized how sex can have life altering affects on people. Sex brings out the best in people, wait let me rephrase that statement. Good sex can bring out the best in people. Good sex can have you waiting on hand and foot for someone. I remember when my wife and I first got serious I started pulling sexual tricks out my hat with plenty of sexual surprises. Over time she would counter all of my sexual actions by duplicating pleasures that I've previously performed on her. Back then she was attending John Jay college and often I would come to bring her a bit more then lunch on her lunch break. Our sexual addictions for one another grew and I was always able to "keep it up" but she couldn't. Her grades and test scores began to drop. I then realized how our sexual desires and chemistry was interfering with her school work. We had a long talk about our short and long term goals and decided to decrease our quality time so she can have more time to study. I tried studying with her but it didn't work. At that time our sexual apatite for one another prevented us from getting any work done. After thinking with my other head we began studying over the phone, communicating from Brooklyn to Washington Heights. Though her sexy Latina accent kept me aroused we got through it together, which contributed to her completing her course with honors and receiving her Bachelors degree, in 2005.

Good sex can bring out the worst in people as well, a friend of mines who's name I'll keep anonymous encountered a similar situation, except instead of him staying focused, continuing his education and scholarship at Virginia Tech. He grew weak for his high school sweetheart in Brooklyn. He loved her so much that he couldn't be without her, at least that's what he told his parents. I was shocked that he dropped out of school and came back to our hood in Brooklyn? I thought how can love at such a young age lead one to dispose of their dreams of becoming a pro football player, so I had to ask. "Why you didn't finish school and try to make it pro?" He then slowly replied shaking his head in shame. "Sheila got the best pussy and head I ever had, and I knew I'd loose her if I stayed away at school playing ball."

Sheila is now married with 3 children by another guy after publicly posting her wants and needs on social media. As for him, he's working dead end jobs barely getting by, single with no children, funds, or friends. When we think about our future goals and dreams, we have to think beyond the sex for a minute, exclude your sexy love affair out of the equation and think rational about your goals in life. Power moves that are not executed because a long distance relationship is not working can have disastrous results. Please don't let good sex distort your mind from focusing on the big picture. Aim for your goals and if the relationship is meant to be, it will work itself out if you put the effort.

How many of us love our jobs? Did you know that 80% of Americans dislike their jobs but they remain complacent because their bills are paid. With the shape that the economy is in today, most of us need our jobs, we can't just quit with the hopes of finding a better job the following week. We all wish it was that simple, but in reality, it's not. Did you know that 7 out of 10, people are late for work do to fulfilling sexual pleasures, which delays their process of being ready on time.

I like morning sex as well, followed by a Boston Creme donut and iced coffee. Though I'm an Entrepreneur what keeps me on time is the ability to adjust to time. Awakening to my sexy wife laying in bed is a turn on in itself. After the first couple times of me being late for appointments, I set the alarm for a half hour earlier. Though I'm losing a half hour of sleep, I'm keeping my wife happy with a fulfilling sex life, and priceless thoughts throughout my day. The key is fulfilling sexual wants and needs to your life, by conveniently fitting them in to your short term and long term schedules.

Is it even time to settle down? Let's not confuse settling down with having a good sex partner that's convenient and loyal for the moment. Loyal as defined by Webster's dictionary is faithful in allegiance to one government, or faithful to a cause or ideal. In this case, when I mention loyal, I am referring to faithful to a cause or ideal. You now have a loyal companion, faithful to being your ideal sex partner. Where you are at in life along with your goals, determines if it is time to settle down.

I use the term settling down as you've found the right one that you want to spend the rest of your life with, that can be added in your long-term goals. Let's say you want to join the Army and your companion gives you an ultimatum, stating that if you join the Army, the relationship is over. Now you know that this person is not someone you can settle down with. You have to first rationalize both of your goals and come to an agreement. That is why it's best to discuss these type of topics as soon as you find yourself dedicating a lot of time to this one individual. Some things need to be addressed immediately, so you can evaluate yourself and know how much emotions and effort you are willing to invest in this relationship. Emotion is defined as an intense feeling (love, hate or despair) this feeling called emotion, must be controlled when it comes to relationships. You have to know whether or not this person is someone you can become emotionally attached to. Are you content with just having a sexual relationship with this person?

Most people misconstrue a loyal sexual relationship with a long term settling down relationship. This is where communication comes in. Though it is difficult to control our emotions, we must not set ourselves up for failure. It's true that no one knows what the future holds but one can inquire to find the most likely possibilities.

It is time to discuss future goals, plans, wants and needs with your partner, to determine where your relationship is headed. Ask if they plan on staying in your local town for the next five years. Ask what their plans are for the next five years. Ask about short and long term goals, their career and where is their ideal place to live? You want to discuss these topics and more, so you can control your emotions and figure out if this relationship is solely based on sex. In the meantime, it's okay to search for the individual that shares the same goals, wants and needs, as you do.

Maybe your relationship is the total opposite! Your companion shares the same goals, wants and needs but the sex still needs work? How much work does it need? Did you try showing them while telling them your sexual desires? It's still not working, but you're not ready to give up yet? Good, that means you possess a great quality that most of us lack, which is patience. Patience is one of the key ingredients needed in life, along with sex, success and everything in between.

Have you tried watching porn to heighten your sexual ideas? How about using a vibrator? A vibrating dildo? Viagra? More lubricant? Whips? Cuffs? Feathers? Chains? New positions? More foreplay? Role playing? Try some of these options first and if none of the above work, I'll give you some personal tips on how to perform my favorite sexual stimulations.

Has the sex gotten better? Are you bragging to your friends and/or some colleagues? Here it comes, "Do they have any friends?" that's the main response from single friends or friends that are not so happy in their relationships.

Is it time to double date? You should only double date when both are secure with themselves and one another in a relationship. The old, "let me bring my friend along to see if they're right for me" doesn't really work. Often, friends are too judgmental, there could be qualities that you like in someone but because your friend doesn't like them, you move on to the next. That's all wrong, most times your "friend" give wrong advice because they're judging the individual on what's right for themselves, not you.

Realistically, how can your friend know if someone is right for you? They could be totally mistaking on their judge of character for many different reasons. Your friend may come off too aggressive, asking all the wrong questions at the wrong time, which creates a negative atmosphere, defensive attitude and lots of unnecessary tension.

The best time for match making and double dating is after at least six months, by now you and your mate should be secure with one another. You should be able to openly discuss many different topics and be able to voice your opinion respectfully. This is when you can bring along a friend, without their friend being bias as well as yours. Lasting six months, shows you were able to figure out on your own, if this person is right for you. If your relationship is going great then the opinion of others shouldn't matter.

Don't try to be a matchmaker, simply introduce the two and you and your mate, proceed as usual. Allow your friends to interact and enjoy the moment. One of the main reason why you don't want to give too much input into your friends new acquaintance, is that usually if things don't work out, somehow it's all your fault. Let them know from the beginning that you are simply introducing them, what happens next, is up to them. You don't want to ruin your great or good, sexual relationship with your partner, for the sake of your friend not making that love connection they anticipated.

If the chemistry isn't there, it just isn't there and if it is, you'll know it. Don't be surprised if after the goodbye hugs, your friend is lip locking with your companion's friend. Often our sexual chemistry between our mates are contagious. Based on the sexual encounters you might have mentioned to your friend that may now be longing for that same pleasure. Commonly friends desire your same experiences, becoming thoughtlessly compelled in that moment.

Often, friends feed off of other friends energy. If you and your mate are very affectionate, kissing and holding hands may create the mood for your friends to follow. Public displays of affection can be contagious. Couples often compete for this romantic spotlight, to prove that they're more sexually compatible in their relationship.

Believe it or not, by you passionately kissing your mate while on a date with both of your friends, you may in fact get them aroused also. It's the same as watching a pornographic movie. Or should I say soft porn. You see the sexual action occurring and now you want this stimulation yourself. It is human nature to see something you like and want if for yourself.

You and your companion's friend may just happen to hit it off, what's next? You should limit your double dating to a minimum of once every other month. If you're happy in your relationship, keep it that way as much as possible. You lit the match, now it's up to your friend to keep the fire going. Don't worry too much about them maintaining their relationship as friends and keep most advice to yourself. You'll soon learn that connecting your friend to your mate's friend, can be disastrous. An abundance of comparing and referencing may occur and you may have to lie as an alibi if your friend is the unfaithful type.

How about not match making at all? Great decision! If you happen to brag to your friends about your good sex life and good relationship, know where to draw the line. Even if it means lying. Did I just say that? Okay, I may be wrong. You don't want to lie about your partner not having friends, just let them know that you're happy the way things are and the double dipping can be hazardous to the foundation that you're building.

I suggest both parties invite friends out for group entertainment like bowling or to a barbecue or birthday party at a lounge or club. This way everyone is mingling and you're not as responsible if the spark is defused. The group approach is less pressure, and the love connection is not as forced as the one on one, highly anticipated date.

Where do we go from here? The relationship is going well, and you're frequently visiting your companion for sexual encounters. At this point the sex may start to become too routine. Now is the perfect time to become spontaneous. I'm not saying risk being arrested for indecent exposure or a racy encounter in that nature, but try new places to have sex, switch the scenery. The worst thing you can do is have the same routine. Along with places, switch positions as well, including your seductive approach.

If you're always passive, try being dominant. If you're always eager and forceful then try being more pleasant and gentle. Prepare to evaluate whether or not your sex life improves, remains the same or decreases.

Are you becoming more serious about your relationship or are you fine with how things are? Do you feel like you don't know enough about your partner's family and background? Then ask! Are your parent's still together? Were your parent's ever married? How is your relationship with your parents? What age were you when they separated? Many people that come from broken homes, often resent one of their parents. This resentment can follow them through life and have a negative effect on how they view marriage, children, family, and sometimes even the opposite sex.

In most inner-city communities Fathers commonly leave the home by choice or force, due to an unfortunate situation like incarceration. Whatever caused them to leave no circumstances justifies abandonment of a child especially their daughters. Subsequent to abandonment some girls grow up thinking that their father didn't love them and they may acquire a hatred for men or a negative attitude towards trusting men. Some women may think that because of their past experiences that men will always leave them or decide to leave them if they have a child. These thoughts sometimes are hidden deep within and we will never know unless we inquire ourselves with conversations that triggers this exposure. To some women, an absent father have a total opposite effect. Growing up without a father for some women means that they don't know much about the opposite sex. Throughout their lives these women haven't had a chance to hear a man speak to them with authority or scold them when they did wrong. Many have lacked affection from a man with genuine concern for their wellbeing.

Often women who's father's have been absent from their lives are fragile when dealing with a man because they never had a man speak to them with authority. These same types of women are commonly submissive and are left vulnerable at times. They tend to fall in love fast, admiring their companion as the authoritative, father like figure they've always yearned for. This type of woman seek passion and commitment, before you cross them, you may wish you had never met them.

The reason I touch base on all of the above is very simple, we must know our companion's. Sexual relationships lead to emotional attachment for some, not knowing your mates background, can alter your future within a blink of an eye. Take for instance a rape victim that hasn't fully recovered mentally. In all actuality, no one fully recovers from a rape as long as they remember it. Some rape victims are just mentally stronger than others, the same as with anything else. One wrong move of aggression, can trigger the thought of a traumatic past encounter, causing this person to unexpectedly lash out. Women are not the only victims of rape and sexual assaults. Rape victims are also common with men who have been incarcerated in state prison's. Please keep in mind that one can trigger a defensive response when placed in some compromising sexual positions.

Take for instance a female that has been kidnapped, blind folded, cuffed in a basement and continuously raped over a period of time before escaping. Though years later she may appear okay on the outside, she may fear a similar situation on the inside. Certain encounters could trigger traumatizing memories, causing her to have a panic attack. Her mate can try a spontaneous act of blind folding or put her in cuffs, which causes her to over react, screaming in desperation to remove such torturing objects.

Some men have been molested as boys but are too embarrassed to seek mental help, which can result in a certain situation triggering this awful memory as well. Though these events are not as common as women being sexually mistreated, we all have to thoroughly research our mates.

Most men will not talk about being raped, molested or even having gay tendencies, to avoid embarrassment. In order to get most males to speak of these matters, you would have to do some investigating first. If your partner is a known felon, inquire about their time being incarcerated. Besides asking them personal questions, you can call the prison where they were housed, set up an appointment and inquire within.

Women and men should be careful where and how they play with those dildos, your man might not just be afraid of trying new things. He might have experienced a traumatic anal and oral experience that he's not at proud of. Prison's across the world have no boundaries. Your companion may just have been forced to perform oral sex on a cellmate at knife point. Another possibility is that he may have been the one inserting his penis into another man's rectum. If your partner always wants to have anal sex with you, this act alone should raise your eyebrows. If you can relate, you should investigate.

Each case is different for each individual. There are some Women that have been raped and now they prefer to be stimulated with extreme aggressive force. Some love to be spanked, gaged, blind folded, repeatedly smacked and choked during sex. Some women became addicted to pain, having the need to be bitten and strangled almost to unconsciousness as they reach their climax, fulfilling the ultimate orgasm.

Ladies, don't be surprised if a man you meet, encourages you to put on a strap on dildo and ask to perform anal sex on him. Some of these men are not at all attracted to other men, though they like the pleasure that they once experienced at one point or another in their lives. We all have a past, but will your companion's past now change your future? To each it's own!

I'm not at all justifying anything! I am simply giving answers based on studies given across the

U.S. Along with testimonies, witness interactions and encounters. We all know some untold stories happen behind prison walls! I'm not writing this book to judge but to inform the naive to keep an open mind to endless possibilities.

Even heterosexual men and women, when serving really long prison terms become lonely and sometimes confide in a cellmate for comfort. This comfort may turn sexual when the lights go out. That's why I stress the facts on getting tested for HIV and other STD's. Let me reiterate, don't forget to perform thorough criminal background checks on your partner. Do inquire about his Bro being his Bae!

We have to know who's in our bed and what their day to day life consist of. If your companion seems to buy you things or always take you places that doesn't fit their alleged budget pertaining to their job description, you should further inquire. Take the day off of work and secretly follow them, it's not stalking, it's informing yourself with a reality check. If that sounds too strenuous how about placing a tracking device on their car or secretly activating friend finder on their phone?

They may work a 9-5 but what else do they do? See if they're going to meet a "friend" you've never saw before or seen entering a suspicious location. At that very moment, call their cell phone and ask, "Where are you?" Maybe even, "Who are you with." Notice any hostility in their voice? Awkward moments causes tension. Though they have a 9-5, they may still be dabbling in a life of crime. She may still be committing credit card fraud, or transporting drugs. He may still be selling drugs, selling guns or maybe even committing armed robberies. How about prostituting? Yes, male and female prostitution remains lucrative. They're just more advanced, soliciting off of the internet instead of on the street corner.

What should you do if you find out that your companion is still living a life of crime? It's all up to you, are you already emotionally attached? If so, you may want to try convincing your partner to stop. Regardless of the nice gifts and vacations. You ever heard the saying, "Crime don't pay?" In some cases it's true. The unfortunate goes away for longer then others, most always get caught at one time or another. Now with extending federal statue's of limitations don't be surprised if an individual is indicted from criminal activity fifteen years prior.

Where does this leave you? Do you prefer them to be there for you to satisfy your sexual, emotional, financial and mental desires for the long term? Or is it just a short term fix? If it's short term then why care if they go to prison? Besides your own selfish desires? An emotional, sexual and mental attachment based on present and future plans, may call for you to try stopping your partner from all criminal activities.

A long term commitment to an individual that's incarcerated, will take a lot of strength, the type of strength one must receive from God. Are you strong enough? Sexual frustration alone can drive one to cheat on their mate. It takes discipline to be loyal while they're free, imagine them locked up two hundred miles away. It would take a lot more than phone sex to keep most satisfied.

The lonely nights will feel endless, some can't sleep or eat for weeks while depression sets in. A few phone calls a day, maybe a couple of hours of hugs and kisses on the weekends and if you're totally committed, maybe they will be located at a prison where they allow marriage ceremonies. If so, then once you're married you'll end up on a long waiting list for conjugal visits. This visit allows you to be in a private room, alone, with your spouse for several hours. During conjugal visit's Inmates are allowed to engage in sexual activities but there are very few institutions that participate. Don't get your hopes up too high, this visit takes a long time to be approved and it is only granted about once every 120 days if approved. Most inmates don't get approved at all do to continuous misconduct and violent charges. So, are you up for the challenge? If not, do your research and find out what your mate is really up to and if it's anything illegal, give them an ultimatum, demanding that they stop or you're gone.

Chapter 6:
If You Only Knew

How much do you know about your partner thus far? One cliche states "what you don't know, won't hurt you" I disagree! What you don't know, can ruin your life especially if you find out too late. So let's make sure we really know all it is to know about the person we share our beds with. Within the last decade, there has been an increase in domestic violence and murders by the hands of one's companion. Most of these situations happen because we fail to research our sexual partners history.

Don't take everything for face value, inquire, inquire, inquire. If your mate becomes irritated frequently, this could be signs of rage that is beginning to store up or has already been built. Those mood swings can also be brought on by a secret drug addiction. Pay close attention to mood swings and negative attitudes brought on by the smallest disagreement in day to day activities. These signs have to be addressed and dealt with swiftly. If this is an individual you are planning to have in your life then seek counseling, and seek assistance. Find out why they are behaving this way. If not, this rage that your companion shows every so often can have dire consequences.

Rage and anger aren't only hidden in men. Lots of women abuse their partner's verbally and physically. What causes these strong feelings of hostility that leads to violence? Maybe she didn't get that orgasm she was longing for? Where is that diamond bracelet that was initially promised to her for her birthday? Small promises that are unfulfilled can lead to huge resentment. One may lash out verbally, calling their mate disgraceful names. He may accept this verbal abuse from time to time. Soon after he acknowledges that the verbal abuse has lead to shoving, punching and threats with knives. Until that one day, she really decides to stab him, maybe in his sleep. Sounds unlikely? Well, it's not. There are several cases in the U.S. where men are verbally, sexually and physically abused by their mates. Men are not always the aggressor, there are those many instances where death by deception comes into play.

Before the problem even leads to the abuse, we all want to notice the signs and seek assistance. You can search online for your closest domestic abuse counseling location and attend meetings with your mate. These counseling sessions are usually free or have an affordable fee.

Have you met their parents? If your mates parents are separated, find out who they are closest to and ask to meet them. In fact, ask to meet everyone that they still keep in contact with in their immediate family. This is how you'll be able to further inquire about your partner's history. Get close to mom or dad, maybe even both. Family often expose secrets about your companion that you would have never thought was true. Mom and dad always have interesting stories that you need to hear, both good and bad! Your partner's sibling's are also good people to question when digging up dirt on your mate.

Once you build a relationship with your mate's siblings, at times if you just ask questions, they'll give you a direct answer. The answer might not always be what you want but as you develop a bond with them. Soon they'll feel as though they can't lie to you. Can you handle the truth? Don't ask questions expecting a certain answer. Before you ask the question, you have to evaluate yourself and ask yourself, "Am I ready for the answer that I don't want to hear." Otherwise, you may end up being the one in the relationship with built up anger, waiting to be released as rage.

Between six months to a year, things may become routine if you let them. This is the time to spice things up a lot more. Remember all your initial conversations you had with your mate? Did you ever bother to write them down? This may be the time when they find out that you're not a good listener or you simply have a bad memory.

Do you remember what excites your partner? I'm not talking sexually! Where does your partner seek excitement? Besides sex, what do they find entertaining? Let's assume you don't remember, or you didn't write any of these important answers down, then ask again. Besides sex, what excites you or what do you find exciting about life? What keeps you entertained? What might entertain you that you haven't done yet? These answers will help you entertain and excite your mate. Surprise them with entertainment and excitement surrounding the areas that interest them. Show your companion that you're not boring. Unless of course they're looking for boring. Then in this case you can do absolutely nothing.

Are you bored in your relationship? Are you seeking more fun and excitement? Communicate these desires, as well as your sexual desires, the two can intertwine you know. I'm sure a night out on the town can lead to a sexy challenge. Discovering places to have sexual encounters while out being entertained is always exciting. Have you ever engaged in sex while riding on the wonder wheel? Or literally, sex on the beach? A making out session at a matinee that leads to a sensational sex act is always a reason for the seats in the very back of the theater. Maybe after the fact, you'll find sex at a museum quite amusing. Try fun, new, exciting places to visit and while visiting, you'll be surprised the adventurous, hidden places to indulge in a sex act.

Warning: Some sex acts in certain places can lead to a criminal charge, so be careful and try to be quiet, it's not what you do, it's how you do it.

Is it time to fulfill your ever fantasy? No, not yet, you want to save some desires for marriage. How many people still believe in marriage? Marriage is what you make it and let's keep in mind that it's sacred. So don't give them all of your hidden treasures at once, save some for after the ultimate commandment. Prove that you can be all they want and that when you're ready, you can fulfill their every desire.

You don't have to have a substantial amount of money to keep fun and excitement in your relationship. Vacations to other states and countries are always nice but if you can't afford it, then make the best out of your city. Research fun things to do in your city, you'll be surprised what you find in your backyard. We often overlook the entertainment that surrounds us because we take our cities for granted. Why is it that most look elsewhere for excitement without experiencing everything our native city has to offer? This type of situation also happens with our companion's. Overtime we become accustom to our mates. We get so complacent that we sometimes take them for granted and begin looking elsewhere for entertainment.

For those couples that can afford the luxury of vacationing to other countries you should be prepared! Sex runs ramped and prostitution is legal in many other countries. Several countries have cyber soliciting where tourist are lured in via internet and with public displays of sex acts. Numerous dating services provide pre ordered escorts online. Easily you can arrive to sexual entertainment awaiting in your hotel upon arrival. So be careful of heavy drinking, you wouldn't want to pass out on your mate and let them wonder off, they may just find them a prostitute.

Prostitution is at such a high demand that it even effects the white house. Back in April 2012 history was made when eleven secret service men working under President Obama Administration were recalled from Colombia. These men were disciplined for interacting with prostitutes that allegedly were brought back to their hotel rooms. Reporters can't specify on the facts that happened behind closed door's but the public would speculate that sexual encounters proceeded after one of the agents refused to pay one of the prostitutes for their services. Maybe if he paid like a responsible businessman, the secret service would have kept this a secret. Not that I'm promoting prostitution, but fair is fair.

In certain Colombian cities, prostitution is allegedly confined to it's tolerance zones but the police officials hardly limit the activity to brothels, according to a U.S. State Department advisory. Prostitutes are available at most hotels 24 hours a day. You can also solicit at bars, parks, and clubs in common known cities, like Cartagena, Barranquilla, and Bogota. What is your city known for? Hopefully not prostitution! But, if you decide to travel to another city or foreign land, do your research on the biggest tourist attraction and try to enjoy all you can while you're there.

Don't let the fun and excitement stop when you come back home, find out about upcoming events that's going on in your city. If your partner likes sports, find out their favorite team then take them to a game when that team plays. Do the same thing with any sports, golfing, boxing, etc. Though most main events are in major cities and the tickets are pretty expensive. Order the main event and throw a little fight night party or head out to a sports lounge, that's showing the main event.

For couples with children, taking your children to the circus is not that romantic of course but you are showing them how family life would be if the two of you were to have children together. Don't always get a babysitter and go out, just the two of you. If you have a child or your companion has a child, suggest that you want to take the child out for a fun activity that fits their age group. You want to know how your mate interacts with children, just in case you're thinking about a long-term commitment.

If your partner doesn't want to meet your child or disagrees with you meeting their child or children, this is a red flag. Remember, your child is a part of your life and a long-term commitment can't go well if this individual doesn't acknowledge your child. How your mate interacts with your child means more than being a possible step parent, you want a responsible companion. What if there's an emergency and the only one you can call to pickup your child is your partner. Though most never plan for emergencies. Emergencies do happen!

Believe it or not our mates almost always become our best friends. Whether we realize it or not we tell them most, or all of our secrets. Well, maybe not all of them. If you are close enough they're usually the first ones we call when an accident happens or when we're having a bad day. They may often be the last one we speak to before we go to sleep and possibly the first person we see, when we wake up. We confide in them to talk to when a problem arises plus they always see us naked. So, if we trust our partner's with ourselves, we should be able to trust them with our child or children. Then again maybe not just yet!

Children are another reason why we must know our mate. Research, research, research! You don't want to fall in love with a child molester, only to find out they were only after your child all along. Sounds sick, don't it? This is a sick world we're living in, so let's prevent situations like this from happening by following the basic advice that I'm giving.

How to introduce your partner to your child? Don't try too hard. Invite your partner to your son's football game or your daughter's ballet recital. Supervise your companion while they help your child with their homework. Let your mate know the things your child is interested in and have them spark a conversation over dinner. Most teens easily figure out when their parent is dating, because most parent's start to frequent the night life and take out food becomes the norm. They now start to inquire by asking "Mom who is he, when can I meet him?" Or "He's so sweet, he bought you roses!" "Is she prettier than mom?" Or "Can she cook as good as mom can."

If your child is at that inquisitive age, then they may be more eager to meet your companion, then your mate is to meet them. These situations are a lot easier simply because the child may be mature enough to ask your partner all the questions they want to know about them. This helps create an interesting conversation usually leading to laugher, after you find out your child ask the weirdest things that can be embarrassing in a childish way.

When your child is at this age, it is best not to have them in the house while you're having sex, if you have no choice, then I suggest you try to be as quiet as possible. At age 8 most children start to inquire about sex, depending on how much t.v. you let them watch, what they watch on t.v. and how often you let them use the internet alone. In this day and age children don't have to go looking for sexual activities to inquire about, it may be right in their parents bedroom. Yes, they can hear you moaning, while that old bed of yours constantly squeaks, don't be mad if you catch them listening by the door, remember you didn't remain silent.

Sexual content is all over the internet. If you share your computer with your child and watch pornographic material then don't leave your child alone on the computer too long. They don't even have to search for sex, pornographic video promotions may randomly pop up on the screen, your child maybe curious enough to watch the clip. This one pornographic video clip, may very well change their life for ever. They might become addicted to watching porn, now whenever you're gone, you can believe porn is on. After watching porn numerous times, it's human nature for children to want to experience this act for themselves. Next thing you know, they're not a virgin anymore, or maybe that's only what happened to me?

I was about 10 years old when I experienced my first kiss. I kissed a girl name Jasmine, who lived in my apartment building. I had a crush on for years, I remember knowing how to kiss from seeing it or seeing couples out in public kissing. My parent's never discussed sex so I knew I wouldn't learn nothing from them but at that age, I wanted to learn more. So my new girlfriend Jasmine and I decided to practice more. Though I liked the feeling of kissing Jasmine, we both knew that it had to be more to it. We talked about sex but we didn't really know how to do it. I would sneak and watch my older brother porno tapes whenever I could and soon became fascinated with sex, so Jasmine and I decided let's try it out ourselves and see what happens. For months we waited for the right opportunity, then finally it happened when I was 11 and she was 13.

One summer afternoon, Jasmine and I snuck up to our apartment building roof top and we began making out, for what felt like eternity. After a while, I tried something I saw watching a porno. I sucked on her breast which seemed to stimulate her instantly and anxiously she palmed my head and moaned, as I continued to lick her nipples. With her other hand, she unbuttoned my shorts and began stroking my erect cock. This feeling was something I never felt before, but I knew it felt good and the timing felt right. I looked up into her eyes and we both knew this was it. She slid her panties down to her ankles and pulled up her skirt, at this point I didn't know what to do next. Somehow we figured out that if I sat down on the steps leading to the roof, we both would be comfortable with her sitting on top. Though she said she was a virgin, she seemed to know what she was doing. She took control of the situation, gently sliding her wet vagina up and down my erection. Instant gratifications was sensational, within minutes of this repetitive motion, my body trembled, my cock quaked and I unconsciously ejaculated inside her vagina.

Jasmine then held me and passionately kissed me, I don't know how but she knew what happened. She knew that she pleased me, the smile on her face I will never forget. Though it took me about twenty more times of that same similar sex act, for me to get the hang of it, I eventually figured out how to please her back.

The sexual relationship that we shared was our little secret, we both enjoyed it and seemed to be addicted to it. I became almost obsessed with sex. Back then I would watch porn whenever while simultaneously masturbating. Jasmine and I lust for one another daily, I would tell my sister to call her parents phone and ask for her because she wasn't allowed to have boys call her. Overtime she caught on to how addicted I became, She would pick up the phone and ask, "I know you don't miss me so you must want some more already!" and I always replied "Absolutely."

The roof was our special place to meet and fortunately for us, we never got caught. We often had sex sitting on the edge of the roof top or my friend Carlos's mother would allow us stay at her place. She knew we were in lust and she embraced us without telling our parents.

Months later I noticed she was gaining weight but not enough to be pregnant so I thought. We couldn't fathom the fact that this could happen, she burst into tears and when she did, I noticed the bandaids on her arms. She quietly uttered, "My mother took me to the hospital and they said that I'm pregnant." I was overwhelmed with that information as well as lost for words. My heart started beating fast and all I could think of was pushing a baby carriage to school, for some odd reason.

That day at Carlos's house, was our last time seeing each other. She said that her father was going to kill me if she told them it was me that got her pregnant, so she lied and made up a story about her getting raped, coming home from school. People in the neighborhood didn't believe it and neither did her parents. They eventually moved after the pressure from the police investigation increased. To this day I don't know if

Jasmine had the baby or not. I tried finding her on a few social networks but had no success.

Parents! these situations can and often do occur across the globe. Let's educate ourselves, speak with our children on sex education and monitor their daily routines closely as they develop. There's no exact age where children or young adults become sexually active. If you notice your child being intrigued with watching sex on television, internet or in discussion then educate them on the consequences, as well as protection. Let them know that they're far from responsible enough to raise a baby on their own.

Is your mate and your child getting along well? If they bond, try to get your partner to inform your child or teenager about sex especially if this is a topic that's up for discussion or needs to be addressed. Preteens and teenagers frequently feel more comfortable talking about sex with people other than their parents. They often have trouble expressing themselves because of the parent-child relationship. At times the child may be afraid of their parent's reaction to their sexual experiences and discoveries. They often confide in another mature individual that they take a liking to. I would say I learned about sex faster than most, thanks to my two older brothers that answered every question I asked.

After Jasmine, I was in search of another girlfriend to replace her. I felt the urge to continue to fulfill my sexual desires without delay. Though months went by without having sex, I habitually masturbated while watching pornographic videos. Until this cold winter night when I got out my bed to urinate and had to wait in line until my older sister friend named Michelle, was done.

She opened the door and I hastily brushed passed her, pulling out my cock and letting go. I closed my eyes tilted my head back and enjoyed the release of urine relieving my bladder. "Sheeeeeeessh, knock me over next time." This unfamiliar voice caused me to open my eyes and there she was, looking down at my penis. I gazed into her pretty hazel eyes, then stared at her breast which partially bulged out of her night gown. "You need to learn how to pee straight first and then worry about these."

I aimed my cock back into the toilet bowl stopping the splashing of urine onto the toilet seat. She rolled off a bunch of toilet paper and waited for me to finish. "You not gonna wash your hands?" Michelle said, as she wiped my urine off the toilet seat. Still in awe I washed my hands then she came closer, sharing the running water. "You kind of holding for a thirteen year old." "What does that mean?" I replied. "Ewwww, gargle before you talk again, the Listerine is right there, don't be scared to use it." I rinsed out my mouth in a hurry and repeated the question "what does that mean?" She smiled and answered, "That means that your little man down there is bigger than it should be at your age and is getting bigger as we speak." I looked down and saw my erect cock sticking out my briefs. I tried to push it back down but it got even harder. "Damn I didn't even do nothing to you why you all hard?"

That conversation seemed to be verbatim as I recall up until that point. I remember it like yesterday, everything she said until she pulled my cock out of my boxer briefs and began caressing it. She slightly pulled it as she guided me out the bathroom. We tip toed into my room, she laid me down on my bed and started kissing and licking on my cock. I fell in love with that amazing feeling of being serviced orally while laying subdued. She stroked my cock with her hand and sucked it at the same time, just as I had seen in the adult videos. Before long, the same feeling came over me, just as it did when I first had an orgasm. I ejaculated into her mouth without warning and she immediately spit it out, but she didn't stop. She kept my cock aroused for moments after my orgasm, which I never experienced before. She then slowly climbed on top of me, sliding her wet vagina onto my cock.

I took off her bra and began sucking her breast as she thrusted her vagina up and down my penis. This experience was the most intense and erotic thus far. Once she climaxed she clutched me tightly sucking on my neck as she quivered in my arms. I ejaculated inside her vagina, feeling more sensationally stimulated then ever before.

The peek of the sensation lasted about a minute, she held me for moments after, kissed me on my lips and whispered "don't tell nobody and maybe this can happen more often." She slipped her night gown on and tip toed back into my sister's room. Moments after I laid there in amazement thinking about how wonderful the whole experience was. I smiled to myself and bit squeezing the palm of my hand to contain myself from screaming.

Michelle and I continued having sex every time she would come spend the night, but she never gave me her phone number. I learned later that she was too skeptical about my sister finding out. My sister never found out but I found me a new girlfriend named Keisha that filled the gap until Michelle came around. To feed our pleasures, we frequently had sex at her house because her parents were always working and her brother was out running the streets.

That's exactly how easy it became to have sex, it just seemed like the norm when I got the hang of it. These sexual acts became common, so you now know some of the things to look for regarding your child's behavior. Please try not to leave teens alone for too long or even unoccupied while at work. It is human nature for preteens, teenagers, to inquire about sex but our jobs as parents is to teach them good morals, principles, responsibility and discipline about these topics.

Chapter 7:
Head Over Heels

How are things going with you and your mate? Are they all you ever wanted in a partner? Are they fulfilling your every desire? Are you all they ever desired? If not, you need to level up! Not only sexually but mentally as well as physically, financially, spiritually and emotionally. Mentally it's time to read more, you must absorb constant information about something other than sex and your job or even your college course that you talk about day in and day out. Now that you have your mate where you want them to be and you plan on keeping them around for a while, make sure they feel the same way about you.

Are you conversing about things that your partner is interested in? Don't be shy, create conversations, ask their opinion on different things. Pick a topic, any topic and ask their view on it. A great place to start is the newspaper, stay in tune to what's going on in the world. No one wants an air head. Stay up on current events, the latest gadgets and technology. Sexy is not just your physical appearance and sex acts. Sexy can be the way you speak and what comes out of your mouth. Intelligence is sexy, vocabulary is sexy. To some articulating sentences using proper grammar can be a huge turn on.

Come up with a topic that you and your mate never discussed, but read and research the topic first. Ask them a question based on this topic, then respond giving every aspect of the subject and observe how partner's facial expressions alter throughout the conversation. If your mate likes science but you don't then learn about it anyway, it's not actual science you're interested in, it's your companion. Find out what fascinates them about science and what category of science they like the most. Now your mate may want to use you in a science experiment and this will be totally up to you, just make sure that it's safe, sexy and stimulating. Maybe you'll even erupt like a volcano.

A stimulating conversation that turns into a debate can be sexy also, when couples disagree and no one is there to take sides on who's right, this situation can only be dealt with one way and that's (sex). Regardless of the topic, you get close to your companion stop them in mid-sentence by pressing your pointer against their lips and simply whisper, "Why don't you apply all that energy elsewhere for now!" They may ask "Somewhere else like where?" Then you direct them down to that area you love to have pleasured the most. Then ask "Do you know what makes me climax?" The second question asked should change the whole mood, leading to a sex session.

The following day continue the same topic that you were on, this time have the facts. If you were wrong, admit to it and treat your partner to something special. The same rules apply! If they were wrong demand that they treat you to something special. Special can be an expensive gift or excitement. Even a priceless sex act can be special. Does your companion deserve something special? Only you can answer that question! Do you think it's time for that oral interaction?

Performing oral sex on your partner should be a treat. Like a special gift that only few deserve. Did you prematurely indulge in this act already? Then shame on you! Just kidding, but oral sex should not be performed on your companion until you are sure that they are yours and yours only. Of course this is once you know that you want them in your life, at least mid term. Midterm is the spot after short term, when you're still not sure about the ultimate dedicated long-term. Think of your companion as a new employee that is in training. You monitor their work, give them their position but they have to get through at least three to six-month probation period until they are considered full time. You don't want to rush and give them a raise, "their raise will be considered oral sex" only for them to slack on their job, start taking longer lunch brakes and coming late to work everyday. You have to monitor their work ethic and let them earn their bonus. In a perfect world one could wait three to six months but in todays society with so much sex on television and the internet we usually just go with the flow. Treating your partner special can really be based on how they treat you!

When they pass their probation period and you're ready to perform oral sex on them, let the environment be romantic and comfortable. Don't rush into it, take your time, act as if you were serving the ultimate dessert. Position their body right where you need them to be. You could either direct them orally, or direct them with your touch. Passionately kiss and suck them from mouth to belly button! Then slowly lick down to the targeted climax point and continue to pleasure orally until that orgasm comes.

Kiss, lick then suck the juices from their body until they surrender to your love spell. Look them in their eyes and make sure that you know that they are pleased beyond belief. I'm not going tell you what you should do next but what I am going to tell you is not to perform this act again until you feel that they absolutely deserve it again. You don't want to spoil them just yet, give them their regular base pay until further notice unless they are working overtime. Taking these precautions is also a part of using the mental and being sexy about it, mentally you're confronting yourself. Sustaining from this special act gives your partner time to figure out what they need to do to make you perform again, which will force them to submit to you. When they finally figure it out, they'll work harder to receive this act because it was so fulfilling and they're in desperate need for more, because you didn't spoil them. Some call it mind games, I call it making your mate work for what they need.

"Physically" The physical form of our appearance is what attracts certain people to us. Your companion most likely was attracted to you physically first. Then as time progressed they became familiar with you mentally then sexually, emotionally, financially and maybe even spiritually. We must acknowledge these different categories of ourselves and maintain each one. Physical maintenance is easier for some, few leave the physical form to the norm. Physical appearance can have sex appeal, elegance, style, charisma and much more. The unique thing about our physical is that it deals with so many different elements combined into one, but without the mental, the physical is obsolete.

Most of us look at ourselves in the mirror every morning. Do you like what you see? Are you continuing to maintain a great attitude, personality and sex appeal? Even though you found yourself a partner? Many people get so comfortable with their partner to the point that they lose interest in themselves. Some stop grooming and keeping it sexy, the total opposite of who they were before they obtained their partner. This common act ladies and gentlemen, is the ultimate no, no.

Don't revolve your life around your partners life and their schedule! Continue to maintain your independence, strive for greatness and make decisions based on your own happiness. Do the things you like to do as an individual to uplift your physical, mental, sexual, spiritual, emotional and financial needs! If your companion wants to join in, make sure it's beneficial to the both of you first, before you make that decision. Or at least make sure it's beneficial to you. Take for instance your schedule before your companion, it may have consisted of going to work then hitting the gym after. Don't stop going to the gym because your mate want to pick you up directly after work before attending their bowling league or swimming class.

Continue to maintain your physical physique as you were, because if one put on a few pounds in the wrong places our clothes start to fit different. Keeping your body tight at the gym is what probably caught their eye or maybe it was the way you dressed to impress. Just because you have your mate sort of wrapped around your finger, don't think that the job is done, you have to maintain these attributes which made them attracted to you in the first place. Continue to wear those form fitting clothes that you wore in the beginning of your relationship. Ladies even if the heels aren't as comfortable as the flats or sneakers, wear them anyway. Dress for the occasion, don't start wearing sweats out to dinner just because you didn't feel like ironing your clothes. Remember all the compliments your partner gave you at the beginning of your relationship? So then you should know what they like! Now continue to wear those attractive clothes, even if they can get a little uncomfortable at times.

What about the hair? Well, what about it? Maintain it, if you went to the hair salon or barbershop every weekend, continue to go. Don't stop because going to pick up your partner's child inconvenience you and now you want to try going every two weeks. Let their child wait and take care of your needs first. You'll be surprised how many people lose their mate due to the lack of physical maintenance that one may feel now lack importance. Continue to spray on the cologne or perfume daily, keep breath mints or gum to go. Continue to wear your accessories or jewelry, and buy those new shoes you want. To help maintain your nice physical appearance, treat yourself to your pedicure, manicure and facials, no matter how much time it may consume. The sexier you stay, the better your sex will get physically and mentally. We'll get to emotionally in a minute.

"Financially" Yes, I know these small improvements take money to maintain, that's why you have to stay financially stable and independent also. Due to the fact that now you may spend more money being out with your mate, you have to stay on top of your finances weather it's work, business, or both. Discuss short and long-term goals with your partner, maybe the two of you could collaborate on a business plan to generate more income. Nothing too big, start small and see how this individual thinks and works business wise. If you're not the business type then continue to work, do more overtime or look for a job in your career field that pays more. Sometimes we get stuck at our jobs without searching for better. Trust me, it does get better!

The more money you make, the more you can treat yourself to vacationing, romantic spas and have more of an exciting relationship. Which is always the best remedy for an exciting sex life! Take vacations as often as possible and travel to different places as much as you can. If you have the companion that spoils you and shower you with gifts, this situation is always great but don't become too dependent on your partner. Be sure to continue to cash your own checks, save and invest. You may want to invest in some stocks, bonds or mutual funds, but before you take my advice, do your own research. There's so much more you can invest in, I'm just giving you an idea to stay independent no matter how good the situation is. You always need a financial bandage, you never know when you might get cut.

"Emotionally" Emotions is one of the hardest out of the 5 categories, to maintain. Emotions are hard to control, mentally you may say to yourself, "I'm not going to get emotionally attached to this person," but your feelings control it all. Yes, technically our mental controls it all but often we allow our feelings to supersede our thoughts once we become sexually active. Commonly our feelings make us vulnerable, we become like little children, needing attention, affection and love. These feelings distort our mental, our thinking capability becomes limited because we are only acting off emotions. Some may say, "How does emotions act?" Technically your brain is thinking, but we allow our emotions to control our actions which at times can be disastrous. When you use your mind to control your emotions you have won the battle, but the power of your mind over your feelings, takes discipline.

Emotions are the reason most people suffer from addictions, and a sex addiction is a bad habit to kick. An intense desire for something such as sex with someone can have ones mind distorted from the facts. Just because the sex is right, doesn't mean this person is right for your. A sex addiction can be a hazard to ones health. Addiction usually affects one sexually, mentally, physically, emotionally, spiritually and often financially. For instance, take an average working family man, who may not be getting sexually stimulated at home. He decides to visit a local gentlemen's club, paying a dancer for sex that night and the next day then all of his troubles seem to have gone away. Even though all dancers are not prostitutes he happen to become fortunate this evening.

He returns to the gentlemen's club the next night, in search of that great sex he encountered the night before. He now finds the female who pleasured him and pays her again to enjoy this sexual pleasure, he feels instant gratification and all his troubles seem to have disappeared. This cycle escalates gradually to five times a week, now he thinks he's in love, his emotions has distorted his mind. Within months this continued behavior causes him to become broke, behind on his mortgage and his wife wants a divorce. He goes to the dancer and tells her he's broke but he still wants sex on credit, she then calls security and this man becomes enraged. This story can end many different ways, which will be bad no matter what. These situations happen frequently because some allow their emotions to distort their thinking ability which allows them to act irrationally.

Don't allow a sex addiction to control your emotions. Perhaps a woman finds out the man she's involved with for six months is married, she still pursues him because of their great sex life and a dreamy relationship he promises her. Time goes by, he doesn't leave his wife but her strong feelings for him "which is her emotions" don't allow her to leave him. The sex is great, she loves him but knows he can't marry her because he's not divorced yet. She grows furious and contemplates how to make him leave his wife. She now has sleepless nights, wishing he was sleeping in her bed instead of his wife's. No other man she's met satisfies her sexual needs such as he does! She grows even more furious do to sexual frustration and becomes an emotional wreck because she can't control her emotions. This situation is already bad and it only can get worst if this woman doesn't seek help.

Both examples of uncontrolled emotions are bad but these situations are common throughout the U.S. and beyond. How can we avoid these situations? The first situation is common, and can be prevented simply by following my advice on researching your mate. If you fully research your mate with all components I mentioned prior there will be better sex in any relationship. With the proper information you wont grow emotionally attached, and if so then you'd defuse the spark before the outburst of flames. Information allows you to prepare, don't set yourself up for failure. Emotions are difficult to control, so before you get your feelings involved by having a sexual relationship with someone, find out who they are. Do you have mixed emotions about your relationship? Emotionally attached? Or are you still holding back your emotions? These are the basics you need to figure out, and deal with each individual according to the reality of the situation.

(Spiritually) When we speak of the word spirit, it commonly relates to religion but can also be used as the energy you have inside you or the energy you give off that surrounds you. It could be a good spirit or bad. In this case, I am speaking on both. Spiritually you and your companion should share the same religious believes and stay in good spirits. In spirituality relating to religion, a couple could part ways over disagreements pertaining to religious disbeliefs.

Religion is a way of life for most, so if one chooses to live their life based on their religion and your religion differ, that is an automatic conflict on interest. From the beginning of the relationship, this issue should be discussed but some of us avoid it because it's a touchy subject. One's family may disown them because he/she may have converted to another religion based on beliefs studied by their mate. Should religion become an issue? You have to choose wisely about your future with your family, companion and the God that you serve, if any.

Should you pursue a relationship with someone you know has different religious beliefs but you're physically attracted to them? I suggest that you seek a partner that shares the same religious beliefs unless you want to try and convert them in the process of building your relationship. Who will pray at dinner time? Who will you pray to at night? Will you pray? Who's religion should your children practice? What religious symbols would hang throughout the house? Which ceremonies would you attend? What about premarital sex? So many issues will be raised because of religion. Spiritual healing of one's mind, body and soul, should be done with a mate that shares the same beliefs. If not you may find enjoyment in debating about each other's disbeliefs. Are you practicing your religion faithfully? If so, it should not be hard to find a person spiritually compatible with you at your house of worship.

Are you in a relationship and it's not working because you and your partner do not connect spiritually? This could be a spiritual sign to move on. Many lives have been lost, do to religious disagreements! Families often won't acknowledge a child born into their own family while practicing an opposing religion. Past and present loved ones haven't been heard from in decades, behind these type of situations. If you are conflicted with this issue please abandon ship before one sinks. Or you can stay in good spirits and pray for the best and in the meantime, enjoy the sex.

Categories such as mental, sexual, physical, emotional, financial and spiritual, are key components in a relationship. All aspects should share one common factor, this factor is that both mates enjoy the same fulfillment of all elements for the relationship to work long term.

As time progresses, your relationship will reach the point where you should determine if it's progressing, regressing or remaining the same. Are you telling your partner the most common line there is in a growing relationship? "I LOVE YOU!" These 3 words mean a lot, though some people say it without truly meaning it. Do you love your partner? Do you think your partner loves you? Do they tell you that they love you? Do they show you that they love you? Do you show your partner how much you love them? Love is expressed many different ways, one may shower you with gifts but is this what you really want? Does receiving gifts make you feel loved? If so, then you should be happy wither gifts. If not then what make you feel loved? Is it quality time? Then ask for it, let your partner know that you need more quality time. Ask them to alter their schedule so that you get what you need. Altering ones schedule to fit in quality time is definitely love!

Do you seek more affection? Are you naturally affectionate? Then lead the way, hold your companion's hand in public, caress their hand or thigh during a movie! Feed them at the dinner table. Give them a massage after work then during the massage ask them, "How good does it feel?" Their response will most likely be. "Real good," then you should instantly reply "I want to feel good too," "Why don't you show me as much affection as I show you, I need a massage sometimes too." This oral reminder will let them know that they are slacking in the affection department and that they need to fulfill your desires, just as you're fulfilling theirs.

If you're not sure that you're in love then refer to the definition I gave earlier in the book, ask yourself do you feel this way about your partner? If not but you're still intrigued by certain characteristics about your mate then give it some more time. No need to force the issue as long as you're content for the moment and that the relationship is progressing, then the love will soon flourish.

The sex is great, your quality time together works for both schedules, your finances are taking care of, you connect spiritually and mentally, you're emotionally stable and your child or children likes your mate. Then what's next? More great sex and excitement! The sex is great but are you getting enough of it? Have you thought about moving in with your partner? Have the two of you discussed living together? Are you ready for this big leap? Then go for it, see if you can take on a new living situation for the better. Though you may find out many new things about your companion while living together, always seek to strengthen the relationship and of course produce a more consistent sex life.

The transition of living arrangements is growth for both individuals this is when the truth will be revealed. You'll find out everything, including what gives your mate gas, how good or bad is their hygiene, do they have a snoring problem, do they talk in their sleep and the list goes on. Are you sure you want to find these things out? Or do you think it will ruin the relationship? Unconditional love will accept any flaws that your mate may possess and even some things you dislike, you can help change.

The love one shares for their partner may help them look pass the flaws and learn to live with it. Also, living with someone will let you know if you're ready for better, for worst or is it time to distrust. You will find out soon enough.

Finding a new place for the both of you to live is the best suggestion. Moving into your companions quarters or vice versa, could force unwanted redecorating. Starting fresh is the best solution, being you both can choose the right fit together from living room curtains to your bedroom color. Did I mention how exciting and fun this whole process can be? You'll learn so much more about your partner and may even get tips on home decorating. Building a foundation together is sexy and fulfilling, once it's all done your relationship should become more meaningful and romantically inclined.

Fortunately for me and my wife, we were both ready for a new living situation when we first fell in love. I was letting go of my ex and moving out of the one-bedroom apartment we shared. My wife was finishing college, contemplating Law School and ready to get from under her parents roof. That's when we decided, let's start our lives together, I was at bliss with this change. I was able to see her more, which led to more passionate love making and I also fell in love with her cooking. What an amazing woman she is! I actually fell more in love with her the more time we spent together, and the better the romance and sex became.

How's your new living arrangements? Is there tampons left in the toilet? Is the toilet seat always up? Is the dishes always dirty? If any of these answers are yes, then it's time to have a house keeping talk. This discussion and any other serious topic is best to have about 20 minutes after good sex. That is if you're still awake. Serious dialog is best to have after sex because if you pleasure your mate the way you should, they'll most likely agree with everything you say. To talk to your companion at a vulnerable time, is always an advantage for you because you now have control over their mind and body.

Keeping your living quarters tidy is always a plus, it's sexy, clean and organized, three great qualities needed for a happy household. Three more great qualities are, having a comfortable bed, comfortable couch and being comfortable with your body. Your companion may want to shower with you, or brush their teeth at the same time you're urinating. The bathroom is commonly shared at any given moment, which sometimes mean you'll be literally caught with your pants down.

Being comfortable in your own home is necessary. You may be too hot and want to prance around in your bra and panties or for men, topless in your boxers, briefs or tight whiteys. Are you self conscious about your body? Exercising more and dieting should help, or just be thankful for what God has given you and learn to live with it. Personally, I exercise 4 times a week and walk throughout my house in my boxer briefs.

Chapter 8:
Addicted To Sex?

The whole building a relationship process sounds quite easy, doesn't it! For most it's actually not. I suffered from a sex addiction and had relations with several women at once, since the age of 15 until I was 25. Freshman year of High School is when I remember, my sexual exploring really reaching a broader horizon.

My sex fetish gotten worst, thanks to Michelle teaching me what sex was really about. I no longer only sort sexual gratification, but I took the pleasure in pleasing my partners as well. Natalie was my first girlfriend in High School, she sat right next to me in math class. Conversations about sex came natural to me, I guess because it was always on my mind. I remember my first words to her were "you need your pussy ate". The reason I uttered those words was because she came to class everyday with an attitude, which was actually sexy but not as sexy as her physical sex appeal. Later I learned that she was suffering from sexual frustration. If the topic of sex came up she often made comments as if it was the most disgusting thing in the world. She always sat with her feet crossed, while clapping her thighs gently together, but the irony to it all was, never once did she seem to acknowledge me. So I figure I'll say something meaningful, sexual and striking to her to make sure she acknowledge me.

The look on her face was priceless and with the smile she gave me, I knew it was true, shockingly, she surprised me in return. "Sam cut it out, you're going to have to come better than that." For one month I never knew that she knew my name. After a few phone conversations, I found out she had her eye on me also, but I guess we just never saw eye to eye. A week later, I was licking her clitoris on her Mom and Dad king size bed. I'll never forget the possessed look on Natalia's face, the way her eyes rolled up and how she gritted her teeth, clenching the fluffy pillows under her head. For what felt like an hour, I sucked on her vagina while forcing my pointer finger in and out of her anus, during this period her body quivered several times, making me feel powerful.

I made sure that I pleased her orally first, then knowing that I would climax just as fast as I slid in, I went to the bathroom and masturbated to the thought of the sex act I just performed on her. Once I released into her sink, I cleaned up my sperm and headed back to the bed. She laid there naked with her feet crossed, half sleep. I licked her nipple to fully awaken her, I kept my cock erect by gently stroking it, then I climbed on the bed, slowly sliding my love log inside of her vagina. How tight and wet her vagina felt was instantly pleasant to my cock, I looked down at her pretty face, she closed her eyes and grasped my back. She pulled me closer, so I passionately kissed her while thrusting against her vaginal walls.

Natalie and I became one, she would change the sheets before our sex acts then change them back before we left. Our sexual relationship intensified each time we had sex. I was fascinated with the way she wrapped her legs around my thighs forcing me into her. Our sex life was great but I was falling behind in school because we started to cut class just to have sex at her place, when her parents went to work. I had to figure out how to pass my classes and keep our sexual relationship constant. We both agreed that we would only cut school once a week, but I still desired more.

Fortunately, Karen in my science class lived with her older sister who didn't mind us having sex most days after school. I remember seeing her sister Tameka shadow sometimes at the door, so I would stroke harder to make Karen scream my name. She would then tap on the door "Karen I hope y'all using protection, we can't afford any babies around here" "We are" Karen always replied. I felt like the man but I struggled with grades and rarely did my homework. Until the day came which altered my life forever. One of my teachers, who's name and subject I promised I'll never mention, asked me to stay after class. She asked, "What's going on? Why are you not handing in homework and failing test?" I looked straight into her sexy brown eyes and replied "My sex life" Her eyebrows raised "What sex life? What you know about sex?" "A lot more than you think, I bet you I could make you have an orgasm by licking your clitoris in less than five minutes." She chuckled then grinned "This is not the time nor place to be divulging explicit content such as this." "I won't kiss and tell" I replied, she grinned again, "This conversation is over, you need to do your homework and study for these test, you're failing." "Maybe you could help me study." "You should go before you're late for your next class".

I started to make my way to the door, "How much you want to bet?" "That was just a figure of speech, but I could match your paycheck." "How would you do that?" "I do a little hustling after school. "Oh, that explains the nice clothes and jewelry, I thought your parents were wealthy, you're a very interesting young man. How about I start tutoring you after school at my place? But you have to promise to never tell anybody, not your friends, parents or siblings either." "I promise, I promise, I promise".

We arranged to meet at her studio apartment in the area of Clinton Hill Brooklyn. I was there at 5pm sharp. She buzzed me in and I anxiously took the steps to the 3rd floor. The schoolbooks were open on the kitchenette table, next to two glasses of orange juice. She locked the door, hung up my jacket and sat down at the table. She went over the class work, explaining in detail the basic information. But all I could think about was sucking on her clitoris. The unfamiliar fragrance she wore was enticing, her voice so soft and sexy, her breast nice and perky. I stared at the pendant of a gold heart, laying between her cleavage as the words she uttered entered one ear, exiting the other. I drank from the glass and tasted a concoction of alcohol, she then gazed into my eyes, smiled and continued to speak.

Moments later I was intoxicated. She left me there thinking about senseless thoughts that led me to drifting off. I opened my eyes and there she stood, in red sequence lingerie. I could not uttered a word, my brain froze and my heart began beating faster. She squatted down in front of me, unfastened the strap between her legs, revealing her red pubic hairs neatly placed over her clitoris. She unfastened my belt, unbuttoned my jeans and caressed my cock. Within an instant, I was aroused. She licked around the head of my cock, massaging my scrotum with her hand. The sensation was intense, I then caressed her large caramel colored breast gliding my pointer finger against her brown nipples. I watched in awe as she fingered her clitoris, then enraptured my cock with her mouth.

She sucked my cock while stroking it with her hand in a circular motion. I felt splendid as I submitted to her sexual seduction. She continued stroking, sucking, thrusting her fingers against her clitoris. "AAHHHHHHHHH, AHHHHHH she continued to moan, rising from below and gently sliding her vagina on top of my love log. She grabbed my hands, placing them on her breast, directing the motion in which she made me rub up and down. She then turned around, up and down her vagina went, clenching my cock as her buttocks clapped together. "Slap my ass, slap my ass" she yelled while resting her palms on the floor. I slapped her ass until I saw my palm print appear, I then gripped her waist trusted forward and ejaculated inside her.

This sexual encounter with my teacher helped me further my sex education. If this had been an actual course, I would have gotten an A+ at the end of my semester. It was a surreal time in my life, I told my friend Pop but I think to this day, he still don't believe me. I couldn't brag about it because I knew someone would had notified the authorities possibly leading to her arrest, and inconveniently ending my lustful affair. The sexual relationship intensified as time progressed, she became more demanding, directing me to tie her up and spank her excessively. I bit her at times until she bled but only because of her direct commands, it started to feel more like work then sex.

June of 1998, I gave up my sexual relationship with my sexually aggressive teacher, after she continued leaving scratches on my back that were extremely painful, especially when I would shower or when sweat seeped into my open wounds. If it wasn't for the pain, I would've remained her sex slave until I was of age to go public and probably had married her. Most females my age were moving at a slower pace sexually, or maybe not, most of my teenage sexual encounters were with older females. What I will say is that I soon became the talk of my neighborhood, by females that were sexually active. I would pleasure them one by one as they inquired whether my high expectation to satisfy was true, and yes I did live up to my rumored expectations.

If you can relate to a sex filled history then you're probably not settled down and married at the age of 39. Or maybe God sent you that special someone that brought meaning to your life sexually, mentally, physically, emotionally, spiritually and financially that you reconsidered. Back in the days I thought I'd never settle down.

Are you ready to settle down? Most would say yes when they really mean no. Sometimes we are content with that one person until something better comes along. Are you just settling until something better comes along? I knew it. You have broken rule number 2 "Never settle for less than your expectations!" More than likely, something better is a no show. Usually we adapt to our mate's flaws and learn to deal with them. Hey, no one is perfect! Then suddenly, you meet that person that you think you've been missing out on, this is where the cheating begins. Are you a cheater? How long do you think you're going to get away with it? Maybe you should just tell your companion, they just may accept it and you'll feel less guilty. Or leave your mate and spare all the drama because this new individual is all you ever wanted in a partner.

Make sure you do all your research first, don't leave your 85 % of happiness, pursuing the 15%. Only to find what you thought was 100 percent happiness is 85 % fabrication. Deception is common in new relationships, it's up to you to get to the truth. Do you tell the truth when you date someone new? About everything? Or just some of the stuff? Try telling the truth this time and see where your relationship ends up.

Are you and your companion getting along at your new residence? Are you loving it? Then give it some more time, don't give up so easy. Practice makes perfect, just like driving a car or riding a bicycle or riding your partner in this case. You came this far, go a little further, see if it's happiness on the other side of the bed. Give yourself some more time to adapt, then if you really can't take it, try to have one last discussion before you leave or change the locks. For freedom sake changing your locks on the door is illegal if your partner's name is on the lease. Is your name even on the lease? You better go check!

Things are starting to run smooth? The sex is exciting? The house is in order? You're laughing and smiling more? You now have a healthy relationship in a healthy environment. Let's keep it this way. Do I hear wedding bells? Only after sex huh, well, that's a start. If you only tell your mate "I love you" during sex or right after, chances are you only love the sex, which can be good, there's still hope. For those that are happy all across the board, did you discuss marriage? Marriage defined in the new Webster's dictionary is the state of being united to another person as a contractual relationship, according to law and custom. 2: A wedding ceremony and attendant festivities, a close union of light and shadow.

Are you ready for marriage? There is no set age or time span in a relationship to get married, there is also no rush. A marriage is sacred and the two should be both ready, you shouldn't feel pressured to marry your mate, it should come natural from the discussion to the question. "Will you marry me?" In America it's traditional for men to propose to women but let me tell you, ladies have been changing tradition tremendously for the last 3 decades. Nov 13, 1999, my ex-fiancé proposed to me, I was 19, she was twenty. She lived with her parents and I had a roommate. Though we had been together for 3 years, we weren't ready mentally, financially, spiritually or emotionally. Sexually! I admit we were wild from threesomes to quickies on a late night, on the side of the road in the back seat of my Navigator. At times I would meet her at her job and steam up the private bathroom on her breaks. Truthfully her oral sex made me stay. Yeah, I took the ring and said yes but the very next day, I had sex with her friend or should I say associate, while staring at their picture together on my wall. Throughout the decade we were together, I was never faithful, but she was worth keeping around.

With all due respect, she was a good woman, I just wasn't ready to commit but I didn't know how to tell her. As the relationship progressed, I moved to Jersey (for business purposes) where I met this sexy, beautiful, Italian young lady that really knew how to treat a man. My fiancé still lived in Brooklyn and she would spend nights on the weekends but during the week Fiona brought new candles daily just so I could drip the hot wax in her rectum as I thrusted her vagina repeatedly with my cock. Doggystyle was her favorite position but she had a fetish that at first freaked me out. She would suck my love log, let me ejaculate on her face, rub my penis in my sperm on her face, lick my anus then suck my scrotum until I fell asleep. Yes, in that same order, every time. I must admit, by the third time, I took a liking to her unusual performance.

Fiona was another one that wanted me to settle down but I was far gone. I was like a dog off a leash but I didn't want to hump legs and urinate on fire hydrants. I wanted just about every sexy young lady that came my way. I had no plans on being faithful. I was selfish, faithless and addicted to sex. I couldn't have a good night rest without it. I would scroll through my cellphone around 8-10 pm making plans with women I met throughout the course of my week to set up appointments for sexual encounters the next day.

Before long I was waking up to different females in bed with me every morning, some mornings two women. I'm just glad that I wore protection and frequented the clinic every three months. To this day, I have never contracted an STD and I'm definitely thankful for not contracting HIV. Practicing safe sex is a must! I learned early on that any instant gratification isn't worth my health and of course not my life.

Studies show that 90% of men that cheat, do it to fulfill their sexual desires, while only 60% of women that cheat, do so for that same reason. Why is sex so addictive? It's addictive because it's an instant sensational gratification to one's self. Some are addicted to drugs, others to money, cars and the list continues but a sexual feeling, when one climax is caused by nature in most instances. Rich or poor, one's human natural desires is the stimulation that comes from sex. Some people have not yet took the time to control their sexual desires.

Have your sexual desires caused you to remain unfaithful? Have you ever thought about having only one mate? Having one mate to fulfill your every desire takes maturity, are you mature enough? Society and most religions teach that one should marry and remain monogamous. "Until death do us part!" In all actuality, most marriages end in divorce because one mate or both, committed adultery.

Adultery: sexual unfaithfulness of a married person!

How hard is it to curb your sexual appetite for others, and remain faithful to someone until death? Extremely difficult! Is it possible? Of course it is. It's all about chemistry and constantly fulfilling all elements in every category, that makes a marriage.

The main components of marriage is not only sexual fulfillment. As I mentioned earlier other fulfillments include physically, emotionally, mentally, financially and spiritual components that must be met. Building on these acknowledged components brings faith, virtue, knowledge, self-control, perseverance, Godliness, kindness and love. These added elements deal with long term fulfillment needed to establish a happy marriage, until death do you part.

All categories combined seems like an unmanageable task doesn't it? Well, it's not easy to maintain but it is manageable. Lets' talk about faith. Faith; allegiance to duty or a person, Loyalty: belief and trust in God. Complete trust. A system of religious beliefs In this instance I'm referring to definitions 1 and 3, though definition 2 should always come first.

Allegiance to someone must consist of, loyalty, and complete trust! Before we wed, most would agree that we must first have faith in God, then ourselves before we can put our faith into another person. Do you have faith in yourself? Do you walk by a extremely attractive person without doing a double take? What are your first thoughts when encountering an attractive person of the same gender as your partner? Do you desire them and momentarily forget about your mate? If so, you're definitely not ready for marriage, you have to gain discipline first, which is basically self-control.

Do you want to learn how to control yourself? This element of one's self is most important but it's extremely difficult. For example, when I first met my wife I was not faithful. No fault of her own, I simply lacked self-control and was immature. Though I knew I met the right woman whom I connected with mentally, physically, sexually, emotionally, spiritually and financially. I was not ready to commit. Instead of being honest with telling her the truth I played with her mind and body. Of course she eventually found out about the different women in my life but she was most pissed about my ex-fiancé whom I used to caused her emotional pain.

Seeing her hurt, I felt bad, I knew that this woman caused me no pain and had been nothing but good to me but yet I deceived her. I continued to lead her on, convincing her believe I was faithful to her and planned on pursuing a monogamous relationship. As far as being faithful it's a work in progress. When she confronted me about my ex-fiancé, I lied again and denied the relationship was on the terms she claimed they were on, and in doing so she stated the most life changing sentence "If you was a real man, you wouldn't have to lie and hurt women to get what you want." Then I thought to myself, what do I want? Sex was the only thought that came to my mind at the time! Suddenly an had! For years I've deceived, manipulated and even scorned many women, all for my selfish sexual desires. I gazed into her teary chinky eyes, glistening off the moon light, got down on my knee and deeply apologized for the emotional pain I caused her.

That conversation made me think like a man, I no longer wanted to hurt women just for sex, instead I wanted to keep this one particular female happy. That was the first time I ever felt sorrow for betraying a woman. She touched my heart, I wiped the tears from her eyes, gently kissed her lips and decided to gain self-control. Though I was not yet faithful, I limited my sex partners to just her and my ex-fiancé. It was weird at first but once I explained to my now wife my problem, she knew exactly what to do. Instead of me having several sexual appointments in my schedule, she took control and consistently called and became aggressive in arranging dates, she was sort of like a telemarketer for sex. She traveled to wherever I was at, and made sure she fulfilled my sexual desires. Each time she appeared, she looked different. She would change hair styles, change eye wear, from heels to miniskirts to catsuits, make up to natural, aggressive to submissive. Each date, there was something intriguing about her that kept me wanting more.

My schedule became consumed with new sex filled activities. I finally found someone that opened my eyes not only with sex, but with all other elements as well. I was also intrigued by her Dominican culture. I still love her Latin accent when she speaks. I also love when she speaks Spanish to me during sex. Initially I didn't understand what she was saying, then once I learned, I was able to comply with her demands.

Are you currently dating outside your race? Don't worry about what other people say or think about your companion, do whatever makes you happy. You only live once and you're living for you, not for anyone else. Being that I only speak English fluently my wife's family's had a hard time communicating with me. I would come over to visit her family occasionally and to this date my wife have to translate most conversation's I have with her father, grandma and several other relatives. In the beginning her family advise her to find herself a Dominican man that spoke Spanish to carry on her family tradition, but she knew that I made her happy so she went with her heart. Though the road was ruff, we're happily married, with a beautiful son and daughter and working on a third addition to the family but none of this would've been possible, if I didn't have faith in God, and in myself to change and be faithful. Though if my wife had no patience which is now a virtue or faith in me over the years of my infidelity none of this would really be possible.

Virtue: Conformity to a standard of right: morality. A particular moral excellence; Manly strength or courage; valor, Commendable quality merit; active power to accomplish a given effect: potency, efficacy. Chastity in a woman; In this instance, I am referring to all six definitions. Are you ready for virtue? Most people love themselves too much, to become virtuous for another, unless the other can upgrade their life.

Morally you have to be ready for a change as well. If you think it's okay to have several different sex partners then your morals are non existent, unless you practice a certain religion where such is permitted along with having several wives. I lacked morals at several points in my life because I had no reason for virtue, your mate should be that reason for virtue. Do you have faith that your companion is worth being virtuous for, and do you have faith that your mate will be virtuous for you? These topics definitely needs to be discussed. You should be knowledgeable in all aspects of the topics listed because marriage contracts calls for it by law.

Again, I'm not suggesting you rush into marriage, that is why I speak about getting to know your mate to the fullest extent before that popular question arise. "Will you marry me?" Don't dare ask this question if you think your partner may say, "No" That means your mate is not ready, you should be absolutely, positively sure that your companion is going to say yes, if you do have enough courage to ask.

If your partner pops the question "Will you marry me?" What would you reply? Mean what you say and say what you mean. A minute after I said, "Yes" and my ex-fiancé slipped that ring on my finger, another female was calling my phone for a sexual appointment. I thought to myself "I am going to hell" How was I going to get myself out of this one? I wasn't even married yet but the ring itself was like a symbol of "I'm taken off the market that is."

This circle of love was ruining my conscious! Before the ring my conversations with women ran smooth, like introduction, compliments, I'm single, call me. After the ring it was introduction, compliments, ring, explain, lie, after lie, after lie, after lie.

It got to the point that I decided to tell the truth because my conscious was bothering me, but when I told the truth, women actually thought I was lying. They couldn't fathom the fact that another woman proposed to me, which led most conversations in an awkward direction. It seemed every female started giving me their opinion on women proposing to men, which was a interesting topic when I was staring into their cleavage admiring their assets! The engagement ring was ruining my player life, well not really the sex itself. None of the women I met really cared that I was engaged, they figured they could change my mind from me jumping the broom. Then I realized how to make the ring an asset and not a liability. So I ran with the truth, "I only said yes because I didn't want to brake her heart, and the ring is actually a nice gift. I need a hug right now, I feel bad" Eight times out of ten, I would actually receive that hug publicly displayed by a woman I just met and explained my ring to, this ring was my new friend. I polished it daily and we went everywhere together, if that engagement ring could talk, it would have cursed me out over and over and over again.

I couldn't believe I said yes knowing I was nowhere near ready to get married until at least another ten years. With selfish intentions, not wanting to lose a good thing, I went along with it and it cost me. Simply because I didn't have the knowledge then that I do now.

Chapter 9:
Wifey Material?

Knowledge: understanding gained by actual experience, information, by range of information. Clear perception of truth. Something learned and kept in mind. All of the above is needed to be considered in a marriage decision. Do you even understand this life long commitment? My many different sexual experiences helped me to understand myself and the anatomy of a woman, which prepared me for my marriage. Had I had no knowledge of all these different sex acts gained by actual experience and interaction with many different women, I might not have appreciated my wife as much I do!

I can honestly say, I never met a woman quite like my wife. She was a virgin that I nourished and blossomed into a "grown ass lady" as she would say. She was nineteen going on twenty and I was twentythree going on thirty. Though she had a previous boyfriend in high school that she had "sex" with, it was considered child's play in both of our books. She stated "I never even enjoyed it, he never took off my bra and sucked my breast, caressed me, kissed my body, or nothing like that. I pulled my jeans down half way, he took a few pumps then it was over before I knew it started, it was horrible, he never even saw me naked, I never had any pleasure at all and definitely not an orgasm, my doctor even told me that my hymen was never broken, so technically I'm a virgin."

At first I thought she was completely untruthful so she can appear to be innocent, until that special night about three months after we met. Being that she's my wife with the honor, love and respect we have for each other I'll keep those details disclosed but like I stated before, she was a "virgin". So pure and innocent, I had no choice but to be gentle, taking my time, passionately caressing every inch of her body. I first kissed her from head to toe, the rest I'll save for your imagination. I will say I made love to her, a never before experience we ever encountered. As I got to know her she helped me reevaluated the way I thought about women. I had finally met a woman out of the ordinary. There she was in the purest form, untainted mentally, physically, sexually and emotionally. That very night I decided that she's the one I'll try to change my life for.

Within months it was a failed attempt. I wanted to change and try to convert into a faithful man now having the first pure woman I encountered but I was stuck in my ways. I lacked self control, I continued to have sex with random women but everything about my now wife, kept me wanting to please her and maintain a relationship with her for time to come.

Do you have self-control? Can you control yourself around someone other than your mate that you are sexually attracted to? Do you find yourself lusting for someone other than your partner? If these things are true, then you might want to reconsider that proposal or you should give the ring back, before things get worst. I found out the hard way that it's better to be honest. I broke my ex heart when she found out that I was having a sexual relationship with her cousin, prior to her proposing to me.

Give me a chance to explain, I wasn't a total douche bag then. I had no idea at first that this female was my ex-fiancé cousin at the time. I met her one hot summer day, exiting McDonald's when she was entering, wearing almost nothing. She had those little short, shorts on with her flat belly exposed and her cleavage on display. Yeah, she grabbed my attention. We spoke and exchanged numbers, within twenty minutes, she was on the back of my motorcycle heading to Coney Island amusement park. We enjoyed a few rides, ate at Nathan's, shared cotton candy until the sunset. We strolled on the boardwalk until she stated that she had never been on a beach after dark. She took off her heels, I took off my socks and sneakers and we walked through the sand down to where the waves came in up to our ankles. I rolled up some marijuana, as we sipped nut crackers, small talking about life.

She smoked, inhaling deeply while blowing smoke in my face. I took the blunt then came closer, gently pressing my lips against hers and blowing a large cloud of smoke into her mouth.

Favielle closed her eyes and inhaled, elevating her large breast then slowly laying back into the sand. She rubbed her hand across her breast and sighed exhaling "Ahhhhhhhhhhhh". I then lifted her shirt exposing her breast and commenced to sucking. As her large nipples hardened, she unbuttoned her shorts and slid them off, unconsciously tossing them to the side. My pointer and middle finger explored her inner and outer vagina as the sounds of the waves splashing on the shore filled the air. My fingers moistened rapidly, as I thrusted in and out of her vagina. "Ahhhhhhhh, Ahhhhhhhh, Ahhhhhhhh" she continuously moaned as she unbuckled my belt then shoving her hand in my shorts. She stroked my cock erratically climaxing on my fingers, as her body trembled uncontrollably.

Favielle shoved me to the sand, crawled over to her shorts, slipping them back on. She returned on her knees and began slowly licking my stiff cock. Her hands held up her body as she remained on her knees, her head bobbed up and down, stimulating my penis with her mouth. She spat on my cock, gazed into my eyes then slurped it up in one motion. She sucked and sucked and sucked repeatedly until I ejaculated. She then sucked out every drip of my bodily fluids and digested every particle of my sperm, as if she was dying of thirst.

I felt sensational, the sand on my clothes didn't even bother me. I grinned staring up at the clouds and thought what did I do to deserve this? Being that my fiancé was still at work, I brought Favielle back to our apartment, where we showered then sexed in the bath. It wasn't until she gazed at our photos in the entertainment center and asked "how you know my cousin?" I was lost for words discovering that she was pointing at my ex fiancé, "That's my cousin too" I hastily replied without much thought.

I was able to convince Favielle that my fiancé was my cousin through marriage, which was a relief to her ears. She stated "cause we were about to be kissing cousins cause I wasn't letting you go that easy." I kept this secret safe with me, and we continued to have a sexual relationship for months until my fiancé introduced me to Favielle at a Halloween party, where the secret was exposed.

My ex-fiancé of course took it hard then I explained that I lacked self-control and that she didn't deserve me cheating on her the way I did. I told her how many women I had sex with since we've been together and she literally almost fainted. I think it was the several shots of tequila she took along with the information she just embedded into her brain.

Favielle and I relationship was terminated. I just never bothered to call and explain but my ex and I, reconciled our differences. I told her I wasn't ready to get married that we were too young and I wasn't ready to stop having sex with other women. Things got even better, this is when I gained more respect for her, she said, "I don't want to loose you, so how about we have threesomes and you stop being so selfish." I accepted her offer and we continued living together. Though we had threesomes, I continued to meet random women and have sex with them up until I met my wife of course, which actually came a couple years later.

At that point in my life, I lacked self control physically and mentally because I had no reason to contain myself nor was there anyone to stop me. Being that my ex accepted my sex fetish, I was able to fulfill all of my sexual desires without hiding them. Come to find out she had a sex fetish herself and that was for women performing oral sex on her while she performed oral sex on me.

Do you have a sex fetish that your partner doesn't know about? If so, you should tell your mate and find a solution. It is best to communicate most if not all secrets to your companion before marriage, so that these secrets can come to light and become open for discussion. Which may lead to preserving your relationship rather than making it a deal breaker later!

Perseverance: "To persist as in undertaking in spite of difficulties."

Some situations may be larger than others! In life there will be ups and downs, regardless of one's financial, sexual, physical, emotional or spiritual state of being. To persevere and overcome these obstacles are often not done alone. If you believe in God then you would know this is why he created Eve for Adam. Though at the time that Eve was created, Adam didn't have any obstacles but God knew that he was lonely, needed a companion and eventually there will be obstacles for him to overcome. Hence in front of every good man there is a good woman, or is it behind?

Most situations will call for your partner's assistance or advice, the choice is yours to take and apply your actions accordingly. After living with your partner a period of time, you will encounter some sort of obstacle or event that can lead to a positive or negative outcome. When this situation arise, you and your mate will have to choose wisely on how the event is handled so the two of you can persevere together. Rough times and difficult situations sometimes bring out the best in a relationship.

You may learn something new and may be able to make a change for the better with this information you just learned. For instance, my wife and I previously lived in a 2nd floor apartment in a four story building in Bedford Stuyvesant. The tenants above us had two small children who constantly ran up and down playing and making noise. We talked to the parents of the children and asked politely can they keep the noise down. Though nothing changed, we stayed positive. We both were frustrated daily but because we were only paying $650 a month for a large newly renovated one bedroom apartment, we coped with it. We continued to save until we were able to purchase our first home. Had we moved because of our noisy neighbors, we would have never found a one bedroom for $650, which was a steal at that price, in that location! We would've been paying double the price which would have set us back a year from buying a home together. Despite the small dent in our sex life some nights, we were patient and eventually persevered. Are you patient enough to persevere with your partner despite the many obstacles that come your way? If not, be kind and let your mate down easy but before you go, you might just want to think things through. Work on being patient and think about the beautiful outcome of your relationship if you choose to defeat all obstacles and persevere.

Kindness: of a sympathetic being or a pleasant nature! Arising from sympathy or fore aberrance deeds. Are you showing a pleasant nature to your partner? Is your mate kind to you? We all should express kindness towards our companion's but not only for our mates, we should be kind to our neighbors, colleagues, friends, associates, even to people who we don't know. Be kind to your spouse, open the car door, in fact open all doors. Women too, if your companion always open doors and pull out your chair for you to sit down, return the kind act. Men need to be treated kindly as well. Maybe some doors are too heavy for your feminine touch? Then how about placing his seatbelt on for him? Yes, a small gesture such as putting your companion's seatbelt on shows lots of kindness and gratitude. It's the small things that count.

It's sad to say, but study shows that the more we become comfortable and familiar with our love ones, the more we lack appreciation for them or for what they do. Their kindness becomes normal to the point that it may go unnoticed. In return, we should be kind regardless because what you put in is what you get back out. How can you expect someone to be kind to you if you're not kind to them? Be pleasant in the things you do, and the things you say. Even if they prefer rough sex, start off pleasant, be gentle, make love, then get rough.

Being kind keeps your relationship non confrontational, when you're in a pleasant mood it rubs off onto others. Some of you may be familiar with the term "kill them with kindness". Of course we don't want to kill anyone, the term simply means be kind at all times even with an "enemy" Don't let them see you angry, upset or down, try to always smile and remain pleasant even at a stressful time. If this was war this is when you attack, when they least expect it. You can make someone that dislike you for whatever reason, take a liking to you because you leave them no choice. You're always kind? How can someone really dislike kindness? Kindness will always outshine the bitter. Say for instance, you and your mate have a disagreement, don't remain angry at them. Instead treat them to dinner and take a mental picture of their face when you're feeding them their dessert. With that one act of kindness they may feel so overwhelmed that they'll be waiting on you hand and foot for the next few days because you handled the situation in such a pleasant manner. Don't be surprised if they just want to perform oral sex on you, wanting nothing in return. Yes, being kind at just the right time can get you what you want and more. Being kind is how you keep your spouse loving you and in return you loving your spouse.

Do you love your companion? Do you know your mate loves you? How much love do you have for one another? Is it unconditional love? With unconditional love often comes monogamy! Sharing the same household often leads to responsibilities, sexually, emotionally, physically, financially and mentally. Commonly we do share all those elements once we decide to commit. Some say marriage is more God's law than it is the government's. Getting married is the Godly thing to do, even if you're Atheist. Ladies I mean you too. So what if you can't afford a ring, there's layaway and financing, saving, or buying a ring within your budget until more money is available to upgrade. How about no ring, just a unity promise, and as we already know you ladies can propose too. Okay let's be honest if you can't afford the ring maybe you shouldn't get married yet because at some point a marriage becomes a business.

Do you have the ring? Now choose an unforgettable setting, some place romantic. How about that special romantic place that you and your mate frequent. You don't have to do this alone, you could get help. Yes, be creative, set up the surprise proposal that will make your spouse heart melt. Maybe a weekend getaway in the jacuzzi or you could propose on a yacht. Either or, just make sure you don't drop the ring in the water.

Your partner said yes, correct? Of course they did. Traditionally, the soon to be bride's dad is supposed to finance` the wedding but since we are living in a nontraditional society, you should sit down with your partner, choose a date, check your finances, make a budget then get to planning. If you're not good at planning events try a wedding planner. Another option is your local city hall marriage followed by a nice reception then honeymoon.

Besides the wedding and reception, make sure your honeymoon is filled with stimulating, sexually gratifying moments. Your honeymoon should be the time and place that you give your all to your mate. Be wild, creative, triple sexy, fulfill your every desire and if possible your wildest fantasy. Try some new positions, do everything that you can possibly think of that involves sexually stimulating your spouse. Don't be shy, suck some toes, toss some salad and please clean the dessert off their body using your tongue only.

What's next on the agenda? More sex and relaxing, your honeymoon is literally the first day of the rest of your life together or maybe until sex do you part. Getting married is the easy part, having a long lasting happy marriage is the difficult part.

You are no longer a sole proprietor in relationship aspect, you now have a joint venture. You are now a team, there is no more I, from here on out everything is we. You are now both equal partners, regardless of who makes the most money. If you didn't sign a prenuptial agreement (an agreement between a man and woman before marrying in which they give up future rights to each others property in the event of divorce or death) or in today's society a prenup can apply to gay marriage. What's theirs is yours and what's yours is theirs, all decisions should be discussed as a team, especially financial decisions!

Though 38% of wives in the U.S out earn their husbands, finances will always play a major role in a marriage. Most choices spouses have to make revolves around money. Money is a necessity, from investing, vacationing, paying mortgages or just shopping for basic households products. Managing your finances as a team will bring out the best in your future. Frivolous spending can cause problems in a marriage especially if you're living beyond your means. You have to now take on responsibilities as a team and disregard the old gender roles. You may make more money than your spouse, but try not to rub it in their face every time there is a disagreement with spending habits. Throw out the mentality that you're the provider and let it be known to your spouse that you're equal by making all decisions jointly. If your spouse cooked tonight then you should do the dishes. If your spouse cleaned the house last weekend, then you should clean this weekend and vice versa.

Are you cooking and doing dishes? Then address this issue, maybe have a weekly or monthly family meeting and mention your likes and dislikes. It's better to eradicate the problem before it snowballs and causes an avalanche. Small issues may unconsciously have you frustrated at times when you're supposed to be happy. In fact, we should all be happy at all times but this isn't a perfect world that we're living in. Marriages have there ups and downs and yes, you should seek happiness but keep in mind that on your road to a perfect marriage, there will be some bumps in the road. Is there a perfect marriage? Your expectations of how happy you will be after your wedding, may be unrealistic. Overall true happiness comes from within!

After the wedding, the reception and honeymoon, it's back to reality which is day to day living. You should welcome and embrace your day to day life and learn to deal with each situation accordingly. Great sex can relieve your frustration when performed correctly. You can relieve your stress and ease your mind by having romantic, passionate, long lasting sex. An active, sexually charged relationship is what keeps frustration away, it curbs your anger, hurt, negative emotions and sadness caused by your expectations that haven't been fulfilled.

After I said I do, I was still unfaithful, I continued to have sex with other women because my expectations of being a happily married man were unrealistic. I proposed to my wife during a time in my life when I was most vulnerable, locked up on Riker's Island for the third time. Where for once I needed her more than she needed me. Out of all my several girlfriends, my wife showed me the most love and she was determined to have a future with me, despite the fact that I was facing a lot of prison time. So when I was released after three months, I felt I owed her for being a good woman to me. I did and still do love her, but I was not ready to fully commit.

My first time on Rikers when I was 16, I told myself to do everything in my power to never come back. Though it was only for thirty days, it was like I checked into hell. I had phone sex with my main girl Darlene, who visited me twice a week and promised she would be there when I got out, but after my thirty days were up, I could've cared less about her being there or not. I was back selling drugs, and partying all while having multiple sex partners.

In 2005 when I was arrested for three different shootings, my wife was with me. The look on her face as I was thrusted into the back of the detective car made me want to burst into tears but I couldn't. I wasn't in no position to be weak. The detectives at the precinct popped corks of champagne bottles and celebrated the occasion, while I watched in awe thinking knowing that I would one day vindicated.

Julie visited me on Rikers the first chance she got, where I explained the situation and she promised to be there for me, and that she did. See the thing is I was never really a bad guy, I never did anything to anyone unless they truly deserved it. For me it was all about Mussy! Yup you guessed it, money and pussy. Defending my honor didn't come easy, not to toot my own horn, but I've always been a handsome go getter. In other words I got money and most females took a liking to me organically. I didn't have to try hard like the ugly bully who was usually broke and masturbated way to much.

While awaiting my fate, Julie went and got my name tatted on her lower thigh as symbol of her love. Upon my release twenty something days later, I had gotten her name tatted on my arm just as I promised, only difference was that my tattoo was a fake.

It took her a few days to realize I hadn't kept my promise when the fake tattoo started to wear off, and when she found out, she was furious. I explained that me and my ex were still together and it would've been inconvenient at the time. I performed oral sex on her and promised to get her name tatted on me in the future and she quickly forgave me. I continued having multiple sex partners but I convinced Julie that I would soon cease and be a one woman man, boy was I lying.

In 2007 I found myself back on Riker's Island for the third time, where I proposed to Julie. The funny thing is she used my cash and picked out both of our rings. We were to get married on Rikers on Oct 22, 2007 but instead God blessed me and set me free three days prior. I wanted to postpone our marriage until we planned a wedding but Julie insisted that we get married on the day planned at city hall. Yes, we did rush into it and I felt bad because the proposal was based on locked down love at a vulnerable emotional time in my life. Most inmates or convicts are lonely, sad, depressed and stressed all in one, so their promises are not genuine. They're not in their right state of mind. While sitting in a cell, most people think about all the things and people they took for granted. For me, it was Julie, I knew she was a good woman but at that ignorant stage in my life, I took her for granted. When I was sitting in my cell with all the time in the world to reflect, I felt bad about misleading her and I wanted to treat her special upon my release.

Once released I did treat her special, I cut off my ex fiancé and minimized my sex partners. Though I cheated, she wanted to work things out so we worked it out and became happily married, but it wasn't easy. We learned the hard way how to be happy. Initially we focused on all the wrong things instead of appreciating all the good. There were days when I picked her up from work with flowers in the back seat and before I could pass them to her she's questioning "Why didn't you pick up when I called you?" or "Who's that chick on your voicemail?" Yes, she had my voicemail code and she still checks my messages on my new phone, but she was never smarter than me. When I met someone I felt was worth me cheating for, I just bought an additional phone which I mainly kept hidden in my vehicle.

Julie stopped complaining about other females as time progressed, while out on our dates she learned to just focus on us. We then enjoyed our intimate time being entertained without arguing. The things we loved to do made us happy so we made it a priority to do those things instead of being upset about my cheating habits.

Maybe cheating in your marriage isn't a problem! Maybe it's money! Evaluate your relationship with money and ask yourself "Does my life revolve around money?" If you're bringing your work home and not paying attention to your spouse because of work related issues, then it does. Most likely you or your spouse may over value money. I'm sure you heard the saying, "Money is the root of all evil" Well that's not quite true, the evil lies with what you would do for the money, in this case I'm asking "Are you neglecting your spouse for money?" Is your sex life is going down hill and you have no quality time for your spouse? If so, these are signs that your marriage is in trouble.

According to research conducted at William Paterson university, a recent survey of 1,700 couples in the U.S. showed that when either or both spouses made money their main priority, they were less happy, and unsatisfied. Let's all magnify the good things in our marriages while solving the bad.

Do the things you and your spouse love to do and make it a priority! Start a schedule, a romance schedule and attempt to have sex at least once or twice a day. Yes, even when she's having her menstrual cycle, if she's if she's in the mood that is. Don't avoid her just because she has her period, if you're squeamish at the site of blood, a candle in the bathroom will limit the light, while you have sex in the shower. Don't make your wife feel unwanted when she's having her menstrual cycle, this is the time when some need your attention the most. Cater to them and try to disregard the mood swings, hopefully it will only last a few days out the month.

Though sex is extremely healthy, especially for married couples, only 1 out of seventeen married couples have sex everyday. That's 400,000,000 couples in the U.S, and only 400 of them are sexually active right now. Enjoy sex to the fullest, have it as much as you can while you still can because as most men get older, they seem to get limp below the belt. This erectile disfunction is sometimes psychological, they lack the romance and the foreplay. Sex becomes more mental as men age rather than physical. The blood doesn't flow through the penis as fast either, or once they finally become erect, if there is no continuous pleasure, the erection may not last long. Or the erection may be there but they ejaculate prematurely. Doctors recommend Viagra and other assistance for those problems. To my Women, just know that it's not over for your sex life if these situations occur further down the line.

If those type of situations occur don't panic, consult your doctor immediately and in the meantime, use some adult toys, your fingers and your mouth. For men that ejaculate quickly, your fingers can help you as well. First you should have a lubricant handy then layer your pointer and middle finger, gently rub the clitoris which is found above the vaginal opening. Yes, at the very top of the vagina! Some women can be stimulated at the first gentle thrust against her clitoris but the right words, caressing of her breast and nipples would be best before or at the commencing of rubbing her clitoris. You would know that she's stimulated by the moistness in her vagina. Glide your fingers gently inside her, flowing of vaginal fluids indicate that she's aroused, this is equivalent to the erection that men get when they're aroused. Men penises hardened as blood flows to the head of the penis and when fully erect, it starts to pulsate. With some women you can actually see their clitoris slightly enlarge and pulsate as well.

A Women's vagina flow with liquids to lubricate their vaginal walls, which prepares the vagina for penetration. Her clitoris (the most erotically sensitive part of her body) often swells up. Her vagina lips then swells and slightly opens, without notice her vagina slightly opens, making room for the penis to enter. Now she's fully prepared for sexual intercourse, but is he ready?

If not continue to rub her clitoris increasing the pace and thrust your fingers inside her, she should now become more aroused, her breast should swell a little, her nipples should harden, her breathing should get heavier, her eyes may now close as she slips into ecstasy, fully charged, hot and stimulated.

Don't stop, continue this same motion, let her grab a hold of whatever she reaches for, no matter how tight she grasps, any second now she will climax. You should kiss her as she sighs, while releasing your fingers. Don't pull them out just yet, let her vagina pulsate on top of them as she enjoys this erotic sensation.

Try pleasuring your wife with your fingers before you enter her vagina with your cock each time, to make sure you please her first, especially if you have that premature ejaculating situation that reoccurs every time you get over excited.

Keep in mind, women can and do exceed men in having multiple orgasms and if you're keeping her sexually stimulated she would want more. So don't think your job is done because she had an orgasm, keep them coming. Though study shows 30% of women in the U.S. cannot have an orgasm, (no fault of the male) I believe different. I know I can fix any problem that any woman is having with orgasms but at the moment I'm happily married so I can't help with that, unless Julie and I agree with this experiment. On the other side of the spectrum, most men rarely have multiple orgasms. Most usually ejaculate, take a brake and if they're real comfortable, might just take a nap. For all lazy men, you need to change this behavior if you want a long lasting, sexually stimulated marriage. The last thing you want is a sexually frustrated wife.

Another idea that men who pre ejaculate should consider is maybe masturbating an hour prior to having sex with your companion. Ejaculating an hour before sex via masturbating is called cheating by some women but for the women that know their mate, do keep in mind that he's doing it for you, to pleasure you longer. The second climax for most men, is not so easily done. While focusing on pleasing your spouse longer and making her have multiple orgasms, your mind should try to disregard how good her moist vagina feels and how sexy she looks. When taken, these steps help the premature ejaculation because you're no longer focused on your desires, you're now aiming to please.

If the fingers don't work for you then try your mouth before and maybe after you penetrate. Yes, of course, keep some sanitary wipes handy instead of that trip to the restroom which can disrupt the mood and lead to a dissatisfied turn off.

Most women love the penetration sensation of an erect cock inside of them and they also love the feeling of oral sex. Because most men think for themselves and selfishly rush into sex, wanting to immediately thrust the vagina rather than pamper it, they often bypass performing oral sex on their mate which is a bad choice fellas. If you haven't yet done so, now is the time to add some taste to your marriage.

First, passionately kiss your companion and slowly caress her breast while doing so. Move your mouth down to her neck and gently lick her throat, then kiss, followed by sucking her neck. While using your mouth to stimulate her, your hands should be slowly undressing outer garments. I emphasize the word slowly often because when taking your time, you build intensity and anticipation which mentally and physically have your woman thirsting for more. This foreplay gets her body ready for what you have in store but mentally, she doesn't know what's next.

If this is or isn't your first time performing oral sex on your companion, if possible avoid the bedroom. Try the living room couch or the kitchen counter, change the scenery, this way she'll have a different mindset and more to tell her friends when replaying the great job you've done. Also, by changing the scenery, it makes this performance more memorable and special. This may be her new place where she wants to utilize your new talent each time. For instance, if you perform oral sex on your wife while she sits on the kitchen counter. Pull up a chair, spread her legs, place them on your shoulders and begin licking her clitoris, sucking her vagina lips, placing your lubricated fingers in her rectum and repeatedly thrusting them inside her until she climax in your mouth. Don't be surprised if she starts to spontaneously call you in the kitchen and you unexpectedly find her with her legs spread apart, sitting on the counter. Smile, you have now added a new recipe to your menu.

For some marriages, being in a sexual mood at any given time is not easy. At this point I recommend that you try using aphrodisiacs a substance that excites sexual desire, sexual pleasure or sexual behavior. Since the origin of sex aphrodisiacs have been used. Back then, aphrodisiacs only came in plant form. The term aphrodisiacs is derived from Aphrodite, the Goddess of love and sexuality. That's right men, I said Goddess, meaning a female God, so please feel free to thank the ladies for the feminine touch designed naturally to enhance the sexual excitement in us all.

Now you can find sexual stimulants in different forms flavors and varieties, chocolate ginseng, ecstasy, oysters, pheromones, stud 100, winter cherry, Spanish fly, love stone, vitamin E, mandrake plants, and the list continues. If you cannot find none of the above, which is highly unlikely, then you can research online to point you in the right direction in where to find aphrodisiacs and how to properly use them to sexually excite you and your mate.

One of my favorite massaging oils that I like to use is jasmine, which activate the smell sense and assist with sexual excitement. Some nights I like using Spanish fly and Jasmine combined, though they are not needed, it takes our sex life to the next level. The combination of aphrodisiacs, romance, foreplay, Viagra, oral sex, and role playing, should most definitely change the settings in and out of your bedroom. Time and patience are other key components to a long lasting, sexually advanced marriage. Don't give up on your spouse, communicate the problem if one arises then discuss the situation and find a proper solution.

Maybe the sex is great, everything is going well then suddenly you suspect your spouse is cheating. What should you do? First off, don't anger your spouse by making accusations until you know for a fact that your spouse is cheating. Why do you suspect your spouse is cheating? Are you just being jealous and overreacting? Prior I mentioned cell phone screening. Your spouse's cellphone will reveal some secret's, or maybe not. Eighter way it's a great place to start.

The best time to check your spouse cell phone without notice is when they're in the shower or sleeping. First you should check the call list, unfamiliar incoming and outgoing calls. If you come across any unfamiliar name whatsoever, whether male or female, you should write down the name and number or store it in your phone.

When you're able, call the unfamiliar number and ask to speak to your spouse, find out who this person is and how do they know your spouse. Yes, be upfront and get straight to the point. This erratic behavior is justifiable, right? If your spouse meets someone new or you ask about their day, they should include this person somewhere in their conversation, don't you think. Find out the terms of the suspected relationship regardless of what sex they may be. Ask, where did they meet? How long have they known one another? How often they see one another? Ask if your spouse mentioned that they were married? Immediately after your conversation is over with call your mate and verify the answers to your questions. If the answers don't add up, leave it at that for the time being but feel free to further inquire.

What about text messages? Yes, text messages are usually signs of cheating, your mate may be so comfortable with keeping their phone on silent or vibrate, so you don't know every time they receive a text. There's so many way's to cheat that I can actually write another book about it, matter a fact that's what I'll get started on next. The real questions are what are you going to do if or when you find your spouse cheating? Wait, why are they cheating in n the first place?

I hope I answered most of y'all questions. If not feel free to email me and I promise I'll discuss it in part 2 and I will also add your answers to following questions listed in "Frequently Asked Questions" You can remain anonymous or get involved leaving your social media info, email, or any other important information as well as your website, relationship status, business, etc. I'm looking forward to the feedback so please keep it interesting I'll keep my answers short and sweet so we can further discuss your's.

Alltheanswers1000@gmail.com @trapsamceph

Chapter 10:
Ask & Receive

Most Frequently Asked
Questions By Women

How do I know if my man is cheating on me? You're the only one that can answer that but here's a few tips to get you started. Does he have two cell phones, a lot of "overtime," long hours at the gym, decrease in sex drive, less sex, less compliments and less affection? Is he spending a lot of time with the "fellas"?

How to make my mate faithful? Truthfully I don't think you can make anyone faithful. People are going to do whatever their heart desires but if you do all the right things that a relationship consist of then add spontaneous acts to the equation, and let's not forget doing the things that they love most. Then faithfulness is a huge possibility.

How to bring out the freak in my man? Do everything to him that you want done to you, then ask him to return the favor!

How do I bring my man home every night? Send him some sexy pics or maybe even a video of you pleasuring yourself, then demanding that he comes home to finish the job.

My man spends too much time with his dudes, and sometimes he acts like he enjoys being with them more than being with me, is he bisexual? I honestly can't answer this unless the dudes he's with are bisexual or gay. Are you sure he's really with "his dudes"?

Should I be suspicious or jealous about my man's Bromance with his buddies? Depending on what type of Bromance he has, some bonds are just unbreakable but if he's treating you right then there's nothing to worry about, unless he's spending way too much time Bromancing and not enough time romancing you.

How do I get my mate to spend more time with me? Entertain them with a sexy strip tease, some good sex, a massage then cook their favorite dish, feed them desert, or maybe eat the desert off of each other. Be creative, role play, fore play, enjoy the night life of your city or spend the day doing the things that they like to do.

How do I get my Dude to perform oral sex on me? Blind fold him, lay him down on his back tie his hands and feet to the corners of the bed, then literally sit on his face.

How do I get my companion to indulge in more kissing and foreplay? Start kissing him more often, especially in missionary and when he tries to stop hold his face aggressively and continue kissing.

I like my breast sucked and my nipples licked during sex but I also love it doggy style, how do I make this work? Start off on top, while you ride, have him suck on your breast then turn diagonal so that the motion of penetration is slightly from behind while he continues licking and sucking, or you can bring another person into the equation to perform either or.

How do I get my man to toss my salad more often? Refer to answer 8 every chance you get.

I've been fantasizing about having a threesome with my man, how do I tell him without making him feel like he's not enough or without him thinking I'm too much of a freak? It don't matter how he feel's it's about you fulfilling your every desire. Let him know what you want and y'all work out the details and make it happen.

My man and I decided we want to have a threesome with another woman, how do we go about finding the right woman to join our sexual experience? You can search online on any dating site or local strip clubs is a good way to find a women that's all the way in.

I find myself being physically attracted to other women, am I bisexual? You probably are just curious but that's normal in this day and age more women are exploring their sexuality with other women because it's excepted and promoted mostly everywhere you turn. In order to truly know you would have to experience it and determine if this is something you want to continue.

I masturbate often, is that normal? Masturbation is normal if you are not being pleasured sexually by your mate or if you are single, many women now have sex toys that they discreetly use to pleasure themselves.

I find myself hot and horny a lot, is that normal? Yes, feeling horny is normal especially if you are in a relationship where you are sexually attracted to your mate and if you are stress free, with spare time to think about sex, and being sexually stimulated.

I would like to try anal sex with my man but I'm scared of pain, what should I do? I think you can start by allowing him to lubricate your rectum and during sex allow him to insert small objects first and over time let him slip his cock in slowly.

I sucked my mans cock for the first time last night but I'm not sure if he enjoyed it, how can I tell if he liked it, loved it or hated it? Did he ejaculate? Did he moan in enjoyment? Did he compliment you? Did he allow you to finish or did he stop you mid-way? Most likely if you are asking did he enjoy it? He didn't. You should know by his reactions to your actions, whether he enjoyed it or not.

What can I do to give my man better head? Ask him what he likes! Or while performing pop the question "Does that feel good Daddy?" While performing ask "You like it like that?" Try different ways to perform oral sex and pay close attention to his reaction. His expressions should guide you to what he likes and dislikes.

I came home early one day and caught my man masturbating while watching porn, what does this mean? It simply means he likes masturbating to porn. Be open minded, play some porn before sex. See if he's more into having sex with you while watching or trying to compete with the Pornstars.

Should I let him know I saw him? No don't let him no just start watching it one day with him, and act natural. If he ask, don't lie. Divulge that you so him but didn't want to embarrass him at the time. He'll respect you and even trust you more.

I fake orgasms at least every other day, is that normal? Yes, it's normal to please your man and act is if he's pleasing you but in the long run you're the one taking the loss rather then gaining the orgasm. Tell him what you want and need and if you don't climax from his penetration suggest he finishes the job with oral sex.

I'm tired of faking orgasms, should I tell my man that I've been faking so he could try harder to please me? Yes and also refer to answer 22 in the process

I'm in love with my man and he's a great provider but our sex life sucks, is it time to cheat? I don't suggest you cheat, you might get caught and lose the providing man for a broke man with good sex. Instead train your provider on doing the things you like done sexually. Guide him to fulfilling your sexual desires. Role play, and foreplay plays a major role leading to your climax. Tell him exactly what you like and how you like it. Make sure you don't please him until he learns how to please you.

Me and my man have two children together but I'm not attracted to him with his clothes off, what should I do? Suggest he gets back in shape, either via gym or buying in home exercise equipment. Encourage him to diet and exercise more often and in the meantime try having sex with his clothes on.

What can I do to make my man be romantic again? Conversation is key in a situation like this, you have to communicate to him that he has become less romantic and remind him of the things he once did to keep you happy. If that doesn't work, attempt to withhold sex until your demands are met.

My husband was just released from prison and he chose to move in with his sister instead of moving in with me and our two children, what does this mean? This means that he doesn't want to be in a relationship with you anymore, but if he doesn't start supporting his children then you should seek child support the best way you see fit.

My man wants sex all the time but my sex drive is in park, what can I do? Try taking a step back and look at your relationship from a distance. What do you see wrong? Or what's missing? Fix whatever problem that is first, then I guarantee that your sex drive increases.

Lately, I've been extremely horny but my man's sex drive has been the total opposite but I'm not sure if he's cheating or just pressure from work, what should I do? Ask him what the problem is? State the obvious and if it's work try having his dinner ready followed by a bath and a massage when gets in after work.

My man like for me to suck his chest, lick his nipples while he's on top in missionary position, is this normal or should I be worried? Yes, it's normal for men to like sensitive body parts pleasured same as most women do, there is nothing to worry about. In fact you should challenge yourself to find more sensitive body parts that he likes pleasured.

My man likes for me to toss his salad, is he a freak or just bisexual? Bisexual is a question of his sexual preference by way of sexual partners, not what he likes done to him. Most men that like the feeling of oral anal sex may feel that it compromises their masculinity but if it's a woman doing it and that's what he likes then I believe he's more freaky then bisexual.

One of my coworkers constantly showers me with gifts and compliments and he knows I'm married but he's just so attractive and I really want to have this affair, do you think I should? This is question only you can answer. I'll just add some thoughts to your decision, how big are you on loyalty? Would this affair affect your job/career? What do you want to gain from your affair? Are you happy in your marriage and most importantly is it worth risking your marriage?

How do I have an affair with my hot next door neighbor, who's also married and not get caught? It's easy to hide an affair, especially when you and the participant are already involved you should just get another secret phone for the two of you to communicate then find time to enjoy one another. The question I always ask is, why are you having an affair?

My girlfriend and I who I've known for the last 7 years recently made out when we were drunk and now she thinks I'm into her when I'm really not, how do I stop her from hitting on me? Communicate to her that you was drunk at the time, you made a poor decision and now that you are sober you regret it.

My man doesn't complete me but he has some good qualities, how do I tell him that I want an open relationship without loosing him? I suggest that you just move on, and find someone that completes you or discretely cheat. No one wants to hear that they're not everything you need. Most people will resent you for that proposal and that's when things will become more complex.

I have a sugar daddy that takes care of all my financial needs but I'm not attracted to him, recently I moved in with him because I needed shelter, how do I ask him to rent me a separate apartment to move in but keep him tricking on me? I suggest that you figure out a way to make your own money and take care of yourself, the more you depend on a man or anyone else to take care of you financially you lose control. If you decide to stay in this situation my guess is that he won't allow you to move out at this point, unless you're paying your own rent.

My man is a great 7 minute man but after he cum he almost always fall asleep, then I have to use a vibrator or dildo to climax, I need help? Try asking him to perform oral sex on you first then allow him to penetrate after you are already sexually fulfilled. If that doesn't work allow him to use your toys on you get him involved. Stop allowing him to fall asleep if you're not satisfied.

I have a male friend that I've known for the past 12 years, he's extremely attractive and I've always had a crush on him and right now we're both single. Should I pursue him? Yes, you should pursue him. Being that you are already friends you have a great advantage. Ask him to join you out at your favorite place to frequent and let your feelings be known.

I'm 35 and I sometimes go out with my niece, age 26 and her boyfriend who's the same age as her. She has a friend that's handsome, fit and has a good job, should I ask her to hook me up with him? Yes, you should pursue a date with him. Though he's about ten years younger don't let the age difference discourage you. You may have a lot more in common then you expect.

My ex boyfriend would suck my toes while he held my leg up during missionary and it felt good and contributed to my orgasms, my new man never did it but I want him to, how should I ask? Simply tell him that you want him to try something new, and tell him what you want him to do to you. I strongly advise that you leave out the part that your ex previously done it to you in the past. He might get offended.

I'm 39 years old and have yet to experience an orgasm, do you think there's something wrong with me? No, not necessarily. Maybe your partners just didn't know how to please you. I suggest you try using a vibrator, a dildo, or maybe start with the vibrating dildo. Find the sensitive parts of your body that you like pleasured and while engaging in oral sex or penetration, make sure that all sensitive body parts are being pleasured simultaneously.

I like to be chocked, smacked and have my hair pulled during sex, but my man that got me like this is locked up and my new man doesn't want to do it because he's scared he'll hurt me, what should I do? Give your new man an ultimatum, tell him that if if can't do what needs to be done then you'll find someone to do it for you. Then give him an opportunity to give you what you need, guide him on what to do, and how to do it.

I want to be handcuffed, bound, gaged and whipped but my husband just likes to give me back shots and eat my pussy, How do I get him to give me what I want? You can either visit a novelty shop that sells hardcore pornographic videos or search for those type of videos online. Watch them with your husband then divulge that you want to try having rough sex. Tell him all the things you want done to you then role play as a dominatrix and demand that he does what you tell him to do.

I've been having an affair with my boss for 5 months and he denied my raise twice, should I stop giving him my goodies until he gives me a raise? Yes you should stop. If he doesn't think your goodies is worth a raise then all thoughts of a promotion is wishful thinking as well.

I want my man to bring home another dude to fuck me in my ass while I ride my mans dick, how do I get my man to fulfill my fantasy? Tell him what you want, if he don't agree right away then purchase a dildo and ask him to slide it in and out of your anus while riding him. Once he see how much you like being penetrated both ways at the same time, he might just come around with a guest for your needs.

I'm a freak, I love sex and I get turned on from the slightest thing, resulting in me having sex on the first date with just about every guy I meet, how do I resist my sexual desires? You have to either learn self control, find a man that makes you happy and fulfill all your sexual desires with him. Or you can continue your same routine if you're happy regardless of what people around you think.

I'm in love with a married man and his divorce seems like its taking forever, should I give him a date to get divorced by or lose us as an item? Yes I think both ideas will work. While you wait for his divorce you should stop all sexual activities with him and also set a date, if he's not divorced by the day chosen then you should lose all contact with him. If you don't set some standards for yourself you may just be forever a mistress.

How do I get my man to leave his wife after what was supposed to be a one night fling? With all do respect if he has a wife then he's not your man, that's someone's husband and in order for him to leave her you have to work 3 times harder to please him.

How do a woman know that she's in love? Whenever any one is in love they feel it throughout their body, it's a strong emotional feeling of bliss, desire, want, comfort, concern trust, any many other feelings wrapped in one. The key to love is to allow your mind to be in control because if not, love can drive you to do things that you never thought you would do.

Ever since my husband and I moved in together, he's stopped exercising at the gym and it's starting to show, how do I encourage him to get back in the gym? You can either offer to accompany him to the gym, suggest he return to the gym or you can purchase some in home exercise equipment that both of you can use while you're home together or individually.

My girlfriend is constantly telling me how good her man fucks her and eats her out, now I can't stop thinking about him every time I see him. Should I fuck him to see what all the hype is about? That depends on your loyalty to your friend and moral standards. Also you have to ask yourself, what do you want to gain by having sex with him? Most likely it will just be a fling and that will make things very awkward between you and your "friend". Truthfully a real friend wouldn't go have sex with their friends companion just because they divulged that the sex is great. You should try finding someone you like that you can have great sex with as well.

I caught my husband cheating, I kicked him out but me and my two kids have been miserable ever since, should I take him back? What I suggest is marriage and possibly family counseling. You both have to get to the root of why he cheated in the first place? Another key factor to consider is how long has he been cheating? and does the person he's been cheating with know that he's married? Does your husband even want to be committed you or did he marry for all the wrong reasons. These are the questions you need answered before you allow you back into your home.

My girl and I went out last week and we exchanged numbers with these two guys who were also at the lounge that we attended. She took the guys number that I wanted, we want to switch numbers, should we? Yes, exchange numbers, go on a date and see where life takes you.

My spouse has a hot friend with a successful career, he works in the same building that I do and throughout the week he's always complimenting me. Should I take him up on his lunch offer? Please refer to the answer to question 51. Also ask yourself are you happy with your spouse or is there too much missing your relationship to move forward? If so then the answer is yes. Never settle for what's on the menu!

My man is over aggressive at times, initially it was sexy but now it has become annoying, how do I get him to relax? Each situation is different when it comes to aggression! If it's interfering with your relationship and if altercations are concurrent in public I suggest first having a deep conversation of what's expected and unexpected. If this doesn't work, resort to counseling.

My man is too passive, I need him to be more aggressive, how do I get him to take leadership in the decision making? Tell him how you feel. Instead of asking general questions, make the questions more specific like. "Where are you taking me tonight?" "When are you going to buy me a new car or can you assist me with my rent/mortgage this month?" or "When are you going to perform oral sex on me?" Whatever it is he's being passive about, you now become more aggressive about! Make him become more aggressive by putting him on defense.

My husband and I have been married for 5 years, but recently I've been getting paid to post different swimsuit lines, lingerie and other products on my twitter and Instagram and he's become overly jealous. Now I'm contemplating divorce, what should I do? If this is your career choice and he's not supporting your career by being jealous and or combative about it your decision making then yes. No one should have to put up with jealous spouses especially when it comes to making your own money. Find someone with similar goals that understands what you want and where you're going with your career, that's going to support you.

I give my man everything from threesomes to head whenever and wherever he wants it but he still hasn't proposed and it's been 3 years, what do I have to do for him to finally put a ring on it? Have you discussed marriage? If not, bring up the topic of marriage and hear what he thinks about marriage. Maybe he's not ready to be committed or he may feel that he's not in a good financial place for marriage. Only he can tell you why he hasn't proposed yet. So ask!

Over the years my husband has become a habitual porn watcher and now he has to watch porn before we have sex, how do I get him to limit his porn watching and get our sex life popping? Have you thought about making porn yourself? You should set up a video recorder yourself and record yourself masturbating with vibrators, dildos and whatever else sex toys you like. Then allow him to watch. Next you should suggest making porn with him, recording the two of you letting loose and exploring one another sexually. After your porn is made suggest he watch the two of you instead of all of the other porn, then repeat this process until your his porn collection is diverse.

I'm 36 years old and I've always dated men but I have been curious about women. So the other night this pretty lesbian hit me up on social media asking me out on a date so I went and yes she turned me out and yes her mouth is amazing but she's possessive and already giving me ultimatums, telling me that I can no longer date men, she's pretty much a man hater. I want children which she can't give me and I still desire a man, should I end this relationship with her now? or try to commit for a bit? I think already there are unrealistic expectations on both parts, she can't stop you from your natural desires of a wanting a man and reproduction. If exploring a relationship with another woman is just an experiment then let her know. Don't lead her on to think that you are done with men and that you are seeking a long term committed relationship with her. Also express your desires to her about having children. Be straightforward about what you want and don't want before feelings get involved.

I've been dating different men for the past 2 years and haven't found Mr. Right, so I've been using dildos and vibrators for sexual pleasure. I realized I have acquired a routine of pleasuring myself and I'm content with that and men are becoming less desirable, can I just live the rest of my life without a man? You sure can, though it's natural to want a man to fulfill your sexual desires and to have as a life companion and partner of many different aspects, he's not necessarily a necessity.

Frequently Asked Questions By Men

Do women cheat more than men? I honestly think that men cheat more then women but when women do cheat it's usually for the better. Women usually cheat as an upgrade, making an intelligent decision to better their situation in which most men cheat just for sex.

Are women more cunning than men when it comes to cheating? Of course they are, most women rarely get caught cheating. Most women usually are in control when cheating. Most women often have the guy/gal they're cheating with wrapped around their finger, on their terms and conditions not the other way around.

Why do most women cheat? Refer back to the answer to number one. There are several reasons why some women cheat, study shows that the number one reason is because their man or husband cheated on them first. The second common reason is to better their financial situation and the third is the lack of romance attention and showering one with gifts just as they received in the beginning of their relationship.

Why do most men cheat? Most men cheat for sex, not necessarily better sex but because someone appealing to them offered it and they excepted or they ceased the opportunity to cheat the moment it was presented.

Why do most women never get caught cheating? Simply because women are better manipulators then men, most women can play coy and men innocent to get what they want and at the same time can become aggressive in persuading their partners to follow their lead.

My girl is gorgeous, has a nice personality, outgoing and career driven but her vagina has moisture problems. Even when we use lubrication she still be dry and complaining that it hurts in most positions. I like to give deep strokes which she hates and she usually wants me to stop before I orgasm, should this be a deal breaker? Yes, if she hates what you like sexually, then it's going to most likely be an uphill battle from here on out. Sexual frustration is on going to lead to both finding sexual gratification from other places unless you are willing to compromise your sexual desires.

I met a woman that is bad and she's a freak but her breath is horrible. I think she has halitosis but she loves tongue kissing me and I hate it, what should I do? Keep some gum or candy in your pocket and offer some on the regular basis. Also you can make a dentist visit with her to see what the problem is and resolve it.

My wife speaks Spanish and she knows that's one of the reasons I married her because I love when she talks to me in Spanish during sex but lately she stopped. Is she trying to tell me something? Maybe she's tired of the same old routine, try taking her on a nice or just a quick three day get away. A night in a 5 star hotel or maybe even an AirBNB. Change up the sex scene, spice up your sex life with some role playing and sex toys, guaranteed she'll be back speaking Spanish to you in no time.

My girl is conservative even during sex, how do I get her to open up? Try some wine after dinner with her favorite dessert. Make sure you eat the dessert off of her. If she drinks more then occasionally the try a beverage with a higher alcohol volume. I'm not suggesting you get her drunk every time you want her to loosing up but you do want her in her comfort zone in a comfortable environment to open up, let her hair down and explore her sexuality further.

I've been taking care of my lady for the last 4 years. Bills, car notes, clothes, shoes, food, hair and nails but because I'm always working to take care of us, I leave her with too much free time, now I think she's cheating. I told her she needs to enroll in school or find a job, so she moved back with her mother. Should I try to get her back or let her go? No, don't try to get her back, you're moving forward and it's obvious she going backwards. She's not conducive to your growth, find someone that compliments you, not just financially but also has goals, ambitions, and drive to succeed.

My wife of 7 years suggested that we set up a profile page of us on a website for swingers. Though we've had several threesomes with other women, I can't watch her being screwed by another man. Should I compromise my feelings and emotions to fulfill her fantasy? If she fulfilled your fantasy why not fulfill hers? If you didn't set the boundaries from the beginning, she may feel that it's unfair to start making rules after the fact. Express how you feel and see where it leads you, but keep in mind she has an unfulfilled fantasy that she may feel the need to fulfill.

Do you think that I'm wrong for putting money over my relationship, pursuing my career as an actor and leaving my lady of 4 years back in New York? No you're not wrong as long as you're actually working on your career and progressing. She will reap the benefits later, but try either flying her out or flying back to spend time me with when the opportunity presents itself.

Where do I look to find the woman of my dreams? I've tried social media, church and even speed dating, any other suggestions? Whatever you like doing for fun is a good place to look, sports arenas, museum's, social events. More public places that have a variety of women to choose from is always a great place. Avoid appearing desperate! Though you're probably meeting potential mates, you could be blowing the opportunity because you're overzealous. Just relax don't search as hard, and eventually she'll fall in your lap.

My wife caught me cheating through text messages and emails years ago. Over the last 3 years, I've been faithful and she continues to bring up my past over every disagreement. She has become extremely jealous and over protective and she refuses counseling and still doesn't trust me. I understand she's scorn but I'm ready to move on, I'm so over it. How do I get her to move on and get over it? Most likely she's not going to let you go that easy, so you have to put yourself in a position of power, find a new place to live and move on. If she starts coming to your work place then you may need a restraining order. If she is refusing counseling then it's really time to move on.

I think I found the one, she seems perfect but we've only been dating 6 months. Do you think it's too early to propose? If so, how much longer should I wait? Yes I think it's too early to propose, if this is someone you plan on spending the rest of your life with then waiting a couple years shouldn't be an issue. Until she starts questioning a proposal enjoy your relationship without the added pressure.

Why is it that most women now of days want only one or two children, compared to the 20th century, where I grew up in a house with six other siblings? I believe there is many factors to consider, but I'll focus on one. For starters most women have become more independent. Most women are no longer stay at home Moms, they are focusing more on their careers and less on an increasing household.

After 8 months of dating a woman previously scorned from her prior relationship, she continues to keep her wall up and I've been nothing but good to her. Should I stop the wining and dining and move on? Or stick around a little longer to see if she's going to at least share her goodies? 8 months is a long time to have gone without the goodies, have a open discussion about the topic and get to the root of her feelings. If she's really scorn or something else traumatic has occurred in her life then I suggest counseling.

I've been having an affair with this woman that knew I had a wife and agreed to continue to be my mistress but now she's pregnant and threatening to tell my wife about our affair. Should I tell my wife myself and cut this chick off for violating our agreement or lose all contact with her, tell my wife she's lying and wait for the baby to take a DNA test? Don't mention it to your wife, your mistress may not really be pregnant. If she is, stress can cause her to miscarriage, and even if she is pregnant there's no guarantee that the baby is yours. Just relax time will tell how it will all play out.

My new girl request anal sex about twice a week but the only problem is when I'm done,

I pull my dick out, seeing shit on the condom which stinks, automatically turning me off. What can I do to stop getting shit on my dick? Make sure she cleans herself well before anal sex.

Last month I went down on my girl noticing a horrendous stench, since then I don't give her any oral sex but I didn't want to tell her why. Should I tell her the problem and if so, how? or should I let her figure it out? If she ask then explain, if not then don't mention it.

I need to make a decision between a pretty, slim model and a not so pretty but beautiful figure, thick and fit in all the right places woman. They both know about each other and they're making me choose, who should I pick? You should choose one or the other based on your chemistry, connection, vibe, sex, goals, conversation and common vale's.

I want to propose to my girlfriend of 3 years, any suggestions on how to go about it? A monumental landmark is always a great place to propose or someplace with a breath taking view.

How do I persuade my wife to give me a threesome? Explain how it will be beneficial for both of you to explore new sexual pleasures, then you can name a few positions that will be most pleasurable if you had assistance.

My fiancé mother, brother and sister are going through a financial crisis and they've moved into our one family home, camping out in our living room, eating our food, leaving messes and being rude. How do I tell my fiance` that either they go or I go? The same way you just explained to us, then add a date to exit by at the end of your ultimatum.

I'm unhappy in my marriage in all categories and after 12 years, we seem to have grown apart. I plan on moving out next month but I feel bad for my 3 children, they are going to be devastated, waking up and not finding me in my bed. What's a man to do? Try counseling, and couples therapy first. If this doesn't work then exit as planned but make sure start co-parenting ASAP or your children will resent you.

My girl has a small mouth and she can't seem to wrap her mouth around my dick and suck it the way I want her to. Is there a surgery to stretch out her mouth or should I just find a chick on the side to give me head the way I want it? Yes there is a surgical procedure to stretch a persons mouth but that is a bit extreme. If she has other great qualities then I suggest you stay with her and sacrifice not so great oral sex. Unless you find oral sex to be a deal breaker.

I got a woman that's smart, beautiful, she cooks, clean, sucks my dick and her pussy is bomb but I never been faithful before. It's like every time I see a bad chick, I got to holler at her, I need some tips on how to be faithful. If your current woman is everything you want and desire in a relationship then focus more on her, start spending more time with her. Plan more trips with her, discuss goals and career plans with her to make sure she's a long-term fit. Eventually you'll have no time left to chase other women because you'll be too busy enjoying the one you already have.

I'm a 37 year old, financially successful, handsome, and fit man. My girlfriend for 10 years match my fly but I'm at a point where I'm ready to start a family. She's saying children will ruin her figure and she likes to party too much to be raising children. How can I get her to accept motherhood and become a real woman? Let her know that if her priorities doesn't match yours, then it's time to start considering other relationship options. Short-term and long-term goals should be planned together or at least discussed. There comes a time when people grow up or outgrow one another.

I'm a Christian man and I've been dating a Muslim woman for the past year. Though I love her, our different religious beliefs cause conflict. Should I move on or try to get her to convert to Christianity? I think after a year you should know whether or not she's even interested in agreeing with some benefits Christianity offer. If she's extremely against Christianity then find someone that have the same beliefs as you.

I prefer fucking my girl in the ass rather than her pussy and now she's trying to say I might be gay but I'm not attracted to men. Should I go to therapy with her on this matter or should I just like what I like? I think respectfully if she doesn't like anal sex but she does it for you then you should try having more vaginal sex and less anal to please both parties.

I'm what you call a 5 minute man and after I nut I can't get back up for a while, so my wife immediately grabs her dildo which makes me feel insecure. I don't like taking Viagra because I'm erect for hours, do you have a solution? Try extremely hard not to ejaculate before she orgasms. Try thinking about something else while having sex, take your time and try not to get over excited. Don't let her dildo intimidate you. In fact you can assist her if your premature ejaculating continues.

Every time I have sex with this woman I date her vagina starts bleeding. She claims that I bring her menstrual cycle down but it's happening too often. Should I get missing now or just consult a physician with her? I think if your relationship becomes more then just sex then by all means consult a gynecologist with her, if it's just sex and you're not enjoying it, then definitely keep it moving.

After having sex with this female I've been seeing for a couple of months, I realized that my bed was soaking wet, like if she urinated during sex. She left soon after as if nothing happened, should I ask her did she urinate on herself or let it slide? Sometimes during sex with extreme penetration some women lose control of there bowels, some more then others. This lost of bowel control can cause urination. You have to decide whether to bring it up as a discussion or not.

My fiance` flew out to Brazil and enhanced her ass and breast, doubling both sizes. I thought she was just going on vacation, even though she said it was a surprise for me, now all she does is take selfies and post them online. She has become self centered, conceited and extremely vain. I admit, her body enhancements look great on her but how do I keep her new body and bring back her old personality, mental state, values and morals? You can't, only she can humble herself. The attention she's getting may have become an addiction. After body altering most women feel more sexy, confident and more in touch with their sexually. She may wear more revealing clothes, and want to go out more as well. This phase that she is going through may not wear off no time soon especially in the era of social media that has become an addiction to many.

ARE YOU OR YOUR SIGNIFICANT OTHER GOING
THROUGH A PHASE?

TELL ME MORE ABOUT IT!

ALLTHEANSWERS1000@GMAIL.COM
@TRAPSAMCEPH

Special Thanks To The Entire Cephas Family!

Special Thanks To My Wife Julissa!

Special Thanks To Jewelle & Sammy

Special Thanks To All Independent Sexy Ladies On Board

Special Thanks To All The Couples That Allowed Us In!

Solute To All The Black Entrepreneurs

Solute To All The Political Prisoners!

Solute To All The Black Men That Will Never Make It Home From Prison!

Solute To All The Black Single Parent Women That Are Raising Children Made By Prisoners Who Fell Victim To The Streets!

CROWNED IMPERIAL TRADING

CROWNEDIMPERIAL.COM

ALL WRITES RESERVED TO:
SAMUEL CEPHAS

WRITTEN BY: SAM TRAP CEPH